LORDSHIP AND TRADITION
IN BARBARIAN EUROPE

Cover Illustration:

An Irish aristocratic court scene of the mid-sixteenth century, showing a lord feasting with his advisors, and his court poet performing for him to the accompaniment of a harper. This is a detail of a woodcut in John Derricke's *Image of Ireland* (1581).

LORDSHIP AND TRADITION
IN BARBARIAN EUROPE

Hermann Moisl

Studies in Classics
Volume 10

The Edwin Mellen Press
Lewiston•Queenston•Lampeter

Library of Congress Cataloging-in-Publication Data

Moisl, Hermann, 1949-
  Lordship and tradition in barbarian Europe / Hermann Moisl.
    p. cm.-- (Studies in classics ; v. 10)
  Includes bibliographical references and index.
  ISBN 0-7734-8151-6
  1. Europe--Politics and government--476-1492. 2. Nobility-
-Europe--History. 3. Oral tradition--Europe. 4. Epic poetry.
English (Old)--History and criticism. I. Title. II. Series.
D131.M654 1999
303.4' 0936--dc21   99-13603
                                                                              CIP

This is volume 10 in the continuing series
Studies in Classics
Volume 10 ISBN 0-7734-8151-6
SC Series ISBN 0-88946-684-X

A CIP catalog record for this book is available from the British Library.

The Edwin Mellen Press   The Edwin Mellen Press
Box 450   Box 67
Lewiston, New York   Queenston, Ontario
USA 14092-0450   CANADA L0S 1L0

The Edwin Mellen Press, Ltd.
Lampeter, Ceredigion, Wales
UNITED KINGDOM SA48 8LT

Printed in the United States of America

To my parents

Herrlichstes Land, erstrahlend in Anmut, überreich an Wäldern, fruchtbar an Wein, ergiebig an Eisen, an Gold und Silber und Purpur; die Männer hochgewachsen und strotzend in Kraft, aber gutmütig und handsam...

Bischof Arbeo von Freising, um 770 AD

TABLE OF CONTENTS

Acknowledgments

'*She koude muchel of wandrynge by the weye*', says Chaucer of the Wife of Bath, and I think I know what he meant. The road to this book has been indirect, to say the least, and on the way I have incurred many academic debts which I would now like to acknowledge: to my teachers at McGill University, in particular Abbott Conway and Les Duer, whose contagious enthusiasm for learning brought me into the academic life; to the distinguished group of medievalists at University College, Dublin, where I had the rare pleasure of working and drinking with Alan Bliss; to my supervisor in Oxford, Thomas Charles-Edwards, whose kindness and good sense rescued me at just the right time; to my colleagues in the Department of English Language at the University of Newcastle upon Tyne for their erudite company and tolerance over the years. Among these colleagues I owe a special debt to Rowena Bryson, who encouraged me to persevere after a disk crash destroyed my only electronic draft of the book, and then restored it from a hard copy. Without her help this project would have been abandoned.

Foreword

This book is about the history of barbarian Europe, but my motivation in writing it was and largely remains a problem of literary interpretation, and more specifically the interpretation of Old English poetry. The essence of that problem is exemplified by *Beowulf*. After more than a century of study there is still no prospect of a consensus on when the poem was written, or where, or by whom, or for whom, or how it related to other poems on the Old English corpus and more generally to the Anglo-Saxon world in which it originated. It is consequently difficult to develop satisfying theories about why the poem was written and what it might have meant to contemporaries, as the plethora of interpretations in the scholarly literature testifies. The failure to achieve consensus on such fundamental issues as dating and localization arises not from any want of trying - quite the opposite- but from a simple lack of evidence: *Beowulf*, like most Old English poems, is pretty much decontextualized. Many literary scholars would argue that this relative lack of historical context need not be a problem, or even that historical context is irrelevant to literary interpretation. Others, myself included, would argue just the opposite. No resolution of that debate is attempted here. Rather, this book is addressed to the latter group -those who regard historical context as essential to literary interpretation, and perhaps even consider that it is possible to formulate plausible reconstructions of authorial intention on that basis. Its aim is to provide some additional historical context for Old English poetry, and in particular about the nature of the oral poetic tradition on which it is ultimately based. It argues that this oral tradition was an aspect of barbarian European culture, that is was politically significant in that barbarian lords used orally transmitted historical tradition as a basis for the legitimization of their authority, that the Anglo-Saxons like other European barbarian groups institutionalized this political function in court poets, and that this aspect of barbarian culture managed to survive relatively long into the period of Christian literacy in several early medieval kingdoms, including the Anglo-Saxon ones.

Preface

This is a book which will prove central to future discussions about two of the most contentious topics in early medieval studies: the nature of lordship and the function of orally transmitted tradition in 'barbarian' Europe. In time it sweeps from Caesar's *Gallic War* to William of Malmesbury; geographically it ranges from the Black Sea to Italy and Ireland; its concerns encompass the traditions of the Goths, Lombards, Franks, Anglo-Saxons, Gauls, and Irish. Yet despite its wide focus the treatment never loses its sharp edge. The argument is carried forward with an engaging logic, gaining increasing conviction as it strips away irrelevance and unsubstantiated hypothesis. Not all readers will be convinced by every step, but there is no doubting the validity of the basic thesis of this tightly-written text.

Moisl demonstrates that several barbarian peoples cherished traditions, formalised in song, which recorded the claimed origins of dynasties or tribal groups, and which gave accounts of notable leaders and events in their histories. Successive rulers used these traditions to justify and reinforce their power by ensuring their own association with these narratives. Crucial to that link between ruler and history was the court poet, whose role was to maintain and transmit the relevant traditions, whilst at the same time celebrating the qualities which placed the contemporary leader within that inherited narrative.

Most of the book involves identification of the peoples for whom relevant documentary evidence survives. This, as all who have worked in the period will know, is no easy task. The evidence is neither geographically nor temporally uniformly spread, and familiarity with its source criticism is not lightly achieved. What is more, there is the problem of relevance. What appeal should be made to the evidence of modern pre-literate societies? Should all references to oral tradition, whatever their context, be included? How far should hypothetical sources behind existing texts be pursued? Moisl's approach to such issues is ruthless but consistent. Not for him the uncritical assemblage: he rejects 'the predisposition to exhaustiveness which characterises research in an historical period where evidence of all kinds is in short supply' and avoids the 'danger of including material not because it is important, but just to be safe'. Rather, he closes in on those 'point-clusters' where there is a concentration of evidence and on individual references which contain sufficient information to support a substantive argument.

Among differing peoples these 'point-clusters' occur at differing historical periods. In successive chapters Moisl weighs the evidence from the various groups, each of which had passed through its own distinctive historical experience. Parts of this analysis are inevitably summary, and occasionally densely written, but the argument is always clear, fully referenced, and authoritative. This progress reaches its impressive climax in a study of the rich Irish evidence, where Moisl's mastery of the material is everywhere apparent.

This group-by-group approach has depended heavily on source criticism to establish the reliability of historical texts. It has also leant on the corroborative method, where the agreement of independent sources on a significant set of features is used to argue for the historical truth of those features. In the final chapter Moisl takes that corroborative approach one step further, marshalling the evidence he has discussed in isolation to establish those features of the relation between lordship and tradition which he convincingly asserts are true of European barbarian peoples in general, whether they belong to 'Germanic' or 'Celtic' groups. Not all of the features were recorded in all of the groups, but conflation of the meticulously assembled material leads to the inevitable conclusion that political authority in early medieval Europe depended heavily on manipulation of a ruler's association with an established national or dynastic historical tradition whose transmission was in the hands of (often highly professional) court poets. Though this method of legitimising political power was well established in pre-literate, pre-Christian societies, it is clear that it was a social characteristic which survived into the Christian period across a large swathe of Europe, including the British Isles (where the phenomenon is particularly well documented).

Though Moisl's main concern is with power and its poetic underpinnings, readers will find much else to provoke them in the course of his study. Some scholars will be disturbed by his comments on the contrasting scholarly traditions in which Irish and Anglo-Saxon literatures have been studied, and by what he calls the 'decontextualisation of *Beowulf*. But Anglo-Saxonists will be stimulated by his approach to that epic and by his interpretations of other Old English works –notably the notoriously difficult *Widsith*, where the observable fact of tense change within the poem is ingeniously exploited. They will also value the clear demonstration of the presence of secular poets in aristocratic settings at least until the end of the eighth century.

In summary, this is a challenging book which vigorously engages with issues that are at the heart of current historical and literary debate.

Richard N. Bailey
Pro-Vice Chancellor and Professor of Anglo-Saxon Civilisation
University of Newcastle upon Tyne

1. INTRODUCTION

a) Aim

In 1961 Reinhard Wenskus published his monumental *Stammesbildung und Verfassung*, a study of the ethnogenesis of the barbarian European population groups who appear in the extant historical sources: the circumstances under which these groups came into being, how they maintained their identities, and the causes of their dissolution. Central to his work is the theory that the evolution and maintenance of *Stammestraditionen*, 'tribal traditions', were essential to the ethnic identity and thus the long-term existence of barbarian European population groups, and that such traditions were typically propagated by *die politisch führende Schicht des Stammes*, 'the politically dominant stratum of the tribe'. This theory has been widely influential, and has never, to my knowledge, been effectively refuted[1]. The aim of the present study is to develop one of its aspects: the role of orally transmitted historical tradition in the legitimisation of lordship within a tribe.

This aim is realised as an empirically supported hypothesis about the interaction of lordship and orally transmitted historical tradition among a range of barbarian European population groups. 'Hypothesis' is here used in Popper's sense of a set of non-contradictory statements which make substantive claims about a domain of inquiry, and which are of such a nature as to be falsifiable by counter-evidence; such an hypothesis makes no claim to objective truth, but only to be consistent with evidence known at the time of formulation[2]. The proposed set of statements is as follows:

---

[1] Especially Wenskus 1961, 54-82; refer also to Hauck 1964; Beumann 1966, 182-3. Wenskus' analysis is disputed by Graus 1963, 185-91 and again in Graus 1965, 313-34. Graus' arguments are rebutted by Wolfram 1968, 473-90. Wenskus' analysis is adopted also by, for example, Musset 1975, 169 ff; Kruger 1983; James 1989, 47; Wolfram (various writings in the bibliography)

[2] Popper 1959, 1963, 1970; recent summary and analysis in Carr 1990

1

- At least some European barbarian population groups maintained orally transmitted traditions which included origin legends and accounts of notable leaders and events in their histories, often in the form of song.

- These traditions could include histories of specific ruling dynasties

- Barbarian lords legitimised their authority by associating themselves with such historical traditions, and by manipulating them so as to justify the current political status quo on historical grounds.

- In some groups the maintenance of historical tradition and its application to the legitimisation of lordship was institutionalised in professional poets. These poets were attached to the courts of the lords whom they served, and enjoyed a high social status on account of the service which they offered. The essence of this service was to publicize the patron's qualifications for lordship, and it had two main aspects: (i) maintenance of historical tradition, and of his patron's dynastic history in particular, and (ii) public celebration of the patron in terms of his personal qualities and of his association with the relevant historical tradition. The court poet's celebratory verse generated new tradition which could be incorporated into the existing corpus, thereby ensuring continuity.

- The cultivation of orally-transmitted tradition and of its political exploitation by lords survived long into the period of early medieval Christian literacy in several cases.

2

b) Scope

i. Definition of terms

- *Tribe*

The concept denoted by the word *Stamm* is central to Wenkus' argument, and he duly devotes a substantial part of his book to defining it[3]. The standard German-English dictionary translation is 'tribe', which the Oxford English Dictionary defines in a variety of ways, one of which bears a reasonable resemblance to what Wenskus intended: 'A group of persons forming a community and claiming descent from a common ancestor'[4]. This discussion interprets 'tribe' in Wenskus' sense of *Stamm*, for which the reader is referred to the relevant part of *Stammesbildung und Verfassung*; compressing the hundred or so pages of detailed argumentation devoted to its definition, 'tribe' can for present purposes be taken to denote a population group sharing an ethnic consciousness based on a perceived community of tradition, where 'tradition' is defined below.

- *Tradition*

In Wenskus' terms *Tradition* subsumes a range of criteria on which a tribe's ethnic consciousness was founded[5]: belief in common descent and subsequent history; commonality of law, religion, language, and social institutions; a characteristic *Tracht* or dress. The present discussion is concerned with the first of these. Specifically, as noted in section (a) above, it examines the evidence for the cultivation of orally transmitted historical narrative by European barbarian tribes, and for exploitation of it by their lords. For convenience, this is henceforth referred to simply as 'historical tradition'.

---

[3] Wenskus 1961, 14-112
[4] Simpson & Weiner 1989
[5] Wenskus 1961, 14-112

- *Lordship*

The historiography of early European lordship is much concerned with the words for barbarian rulers in documentary sources: those used in Graeco-Roman texts, those used by the barbarians themselves, how the Graeco-Roman terms can be mapped onto the barbarian ones, and the political structures to which they refer at different times and places[6]. *Lordship* is here intended and used throughout as a general term to cover them all, and can be taken to refer to an individual exercising some sort of authority over others.

- *Barbarian Europe*

In colloquial English usage, 'barbarian' includes in its semantic field: ignorant of or antithetical to stable social, political, and economic structures; illiterate; insensitive; violent and destructive; stupid; dirty. On these criteria, Europe has been barbarian to greater or lesser degrees throughout its history, and the field of inquiry remains unmanageably large. The definition intended by this study is, rather, the one which originated in Antiquity, and more particularly among the Greeks, who took the view that to be a barbarian was not to be Greek, that is, to be outside the community of race, language, religion, law, and culture which constituted the Greek ethnic consciousness, and therefore to be inferior in these respects; the Romans later thought it fair to include themselves in the charmed circle and, for the duration of the Empire, barbarianism was the condition of being unassimilated to the civilisation of the Graeco-Roman world[7].

This latter definition has temporal and geographical implications for what is meant by 'barbarian Europe'. These can usefully be partitioned into three phases[8]. In the first, from prehistory until the expansion of Roman control north of the Alps, barbarian Europe was everything apart from the northern

---

[6] See James 1988 for a recent exposition of the problem

[7] On the definition of barbarianism see Jones 1971; Dauge 1981; Rugullis 1992; Richter 1994, 4 ff

shore of the Mediterranean basin. During the second phase, up to the period of large-scale Germanic settlements in imperial territory in the fourth, fifth, and sixth centuries, barbarianism retreated before advancing Roman borders, and at the height of the Empire comprised peripheral parts of Spain, Gaul, Britain, Ireland, and Scandinavia to the north and west, and continental Europe east of the Rhine and north of the Danube. And, during the third phase, the barbarianism which had established itself in the western Empire via the Germanic settlements was gradually eroded by the re-emergence, during the early medieval centuries, of at least some of the things that had always distinguished the barbarian from the civilised Graeco-Roman --the stable political, social, and economic structures, together with the literacy which subserved these things.

The neat distinction assumed in the preceding paragraph between barbarian and Graeco-Roman during the first and more especially the second phases is, of course, only an approximation[9]. We know that the Romans settled barbarian peoples inside imperial territory as buffer states; barbarians regularly served in the Roman army and later returned home, in some cases to lead their peoples; trade routes from the civilised south deep into the barbarian north are known to have existed from prehistory. In other words, the search for a 'pure' barbarian culture free of Mediterranean influence --a preoccupation in much of the older historiography-- is hopeless. The actual situation was just too complicated to allow us, at this remove, to say what was originally barbarian, whatever that means, and what came north with the returnees or on merchants' wagons with the amphorae of wine[10]. That said, however, it is possible to overstate the significance of Mediterranean influence on barbarian culture. An ex-legionary northern European aristocrat, gone back home and

---

[8] For a recent overview of barbarian Europe see Cunliffe 1988
[9] For what follows see Musset 1975, 162 ff.; Todd 1987, ch. 1; Cunliffe 1979; Goffart 1980; Wolfram 1983a and 1983b; Cunliffe 1988
[10] For this see especially Goffart 1980

now leader of a war band, illiterate and fond of wine, was not a Roman; 'barbarian' remains a valid concept.

An allied problem is determining when barbarianism ends, if indeed it does, in phase three. On any reasonable definition of civilisation, the early medieval centuries mark a progression towards it; when, and given the regionalism of the period, where, can a study devoted to an aspect of barbarian Europe draw the line and say: 'Barbarianism ends here'? Charlemagne's coronation as Holy Roman Emperor, and all it stood for, is merely symbolic. The truth is that no such line can be drawn. One has to be content with noting that, at various times and places in these centuries, certain features characteristic of earlier times still obtained[11]. But historical tradition was orally cultivated by professional poets such as the *spilman* and *jongleur* of continental Europe and the Irish *bard* long into the high and indeed late Middle Ages[12], and there is no obvious watershed separating them from their early medieval counterparts, which raises the practical problem of when to terminate this investigation. There does appear to be a general consensus among historians that most of Europe after about 1000 AD cannot reasonably be described as barbarian in the sense that many aspects of northern Europe in the early medieval centuries and before can, and this offers a vaguely principled terminal date. The motivation for stopping the investigation at c.1000 AD is mainly pragmatic, however: I am insufficiently familiar with the relevant documentary sources and historiography to take the discussion beyond that date competently.

ii. The evidence

We are concerned with the earliest period of European history, and as such the evidence used as empirical support for the hypothesis about the interaction of lordship and orally transmitted historical tradition in (1.a) above will be

---

[11] Richter 1994, chs. 1 and 2
[12] Richter 1994; P. Breatnach 1983; McCone 1990, 27 ff

neither as plentiful, informative, nor as geographically or temporally unifom as one would like it to be. For the subject of this study the primary evidence must be documentary. Surveying it, one finds little or nothing for most of Europe throughout most of the period in question. None survives for the prehistoric period by definition. For the historical period, what does survive relates to the two main European linguistic groups, the Celts and the Germans, and it is unevenly distributed in time and space, which means that one has to collect and assess the available material wherever it happens to lie. Over and above this, moreover, there is the problem of knowing where to draw the line --what to include, what not, and why not. There are some well known passages which are routinely quoted in discussions of early European vernacular literature in general, and which are self-evidently relevant to the subject of this book -- Tacitus' reference to Germanic *carmina antiqua,* for example, or Alcuin's letter to the abbot of Lindisfarne about the singing of barbarian songs in the monastic hall. These and others like them are duly included here. So is less well known but no less relevant material. The problems arise with respect to more marginal evidence. There is no shortage of documentary references to oral tradition in general, to *carmina* and *fabula* in common circulation or simply unattributed; there are medieval vernacular texts, above all *Heldensage,* 'heroic legend', which clearly depend on earlier, orally transmitted tradition; there is Latin historiography which incorporates narratives that to greater or lesser degrees of probability derive from vernacular oral tradition, and whose authors may or may not explicitly cite their sources. Given the predisposition to exhaustiveness which characterizes research in an historical period where evidence of all kinds is in short supply, one is in constant danger of including material not because it is important to the current argument, but just to be safe.

The textual references on which this study is based can be thought of as points on a two-dimensional surface whose axes are time and place: over most of the surface there is a sparse random scatter, but there are also point-clusters which correspond to concentrations of evidence. This study focuses on the clusters and on individual references which happen to contain enough information to support substantive argumentation. What remains may or may not be used in a supporting role in the course of discussion, as appropriate, which means both that this book is not an exhaustive survey of the evidence for oral tradition in barbarian Europe, and that some barbarian peoples are not mentioned at all simply because such evidence as exists for them is in my judgment too marginal for anything usefully relevant to the theme of this book to be built on it. The aim is not to compile a comprehensive inventory of textual materials; this has to a large extent already been done as part of Richter's study[13] of oral culture in medieval Europe. Rather, it is empirically to support an hypothesis about a specific aspect of that culture. Needless to say, evidence that is judged to be not worth using is not being suppressed. A notable example is Widukind of Corvey's later tenth-century Saxon history, whose narrative is standardly regarded in the scholarly literature as incorporating extensive *Heldensage*-type oral tradition[14]. I have found no evidence that this tradition was exploited by lords, however, and so have not included it. To my knowledge, none of the unused material contradicts the hypothesis being proposed here, but it is available to anyone who wants to attempt falsification.

iii. Authorial competence

One can't know everything, even about apparently restricted subject domains, and I am no exception:

---

[13] Richter 1994
[14] Hirsch 1935; discussed in Richter 1994, 175-178

8

- There is documentary evidence for certain Celtic and Germanic peoples which is readily available and really ought to be included in this study, but which is left out simply because I am both incompetent to deal with the original texts and insufficiently versed in the scholarly literatures associated with them. Specifically, this study deals, in the Celtic sphere, with Gaul and Ireland but not Wales, and in the Germanic with the Anglo-Saxons and several Continental Germanic peoples, but not Scandinavia.

- The cultivation of historical tradition and its political exploitation by lords is attested for numerous non-literate societies at different times and places throughout the world[15], which indicates an anthropological universal. It would, therefore, be possible to corroborate and enhance the evidence for barbarian Europe using such comparative evidence. More radically, the anthropological results could be used structurally as a paradigm within which the European evidence is interpreted. But I am not an anthropologist. The aim here will be to provide an account of the situation in barbarian Europe that stands on its own merits; anthropological evidence is used opportunistically and sparingly in the course of the discussion, but it becomes crucial in the Conclusion.

c) Methodology

A variety of academic disciplines is directly or indirectly concerned with the interpretation of text, among them philosophy of language, epistemology, linguistics, literary critical theory, and, most recently, cognitive science. Because it is based exclusively on documentary material, the issues raised by these disciplines

---

[15] For example Opland 1980b; Nyberg 1985; Vansina 1985; Foley 1988; Richter 1994 ch. 4

with regard to textual interpretation are relevant to this study[16]. For present purposes these issues boil down to two fundamental problems:

- How can canonical linguistic meaning be extracted from text?
- How does that meaning relate to actual states of the world?

Most of the historiography on barbarian and early medieval Europe makes no explicit reference to questions of this sort, and assumes in a reader a common and implicit set of assumptions about textual interpretation[17]. The temptation here is to do likewise. It is, however, best to be clear about what one thinks one is doing, and where the methodological weaknesses lie.

The first of the above issues is extremely complex, and an adequate discussion of it would swamp the proper subject of this book. It will therefore simply be sidestepped with the observation that, whatever the linguistic, philosophical, and ultimately cognitive theoretical problems attendant on interpretation of text, all the empirical evidence indicates that general agreement among readers of any given text is not only possible but is in fact the default case: real-world political, economic, legal, and commercial structures function more or less successfully, and this successful functioning in very large part depends on general agreement about the meaning of text. Some discussion of the relationship between textual meaning and states of the world is necessary, however.

In text with contemporary reference, the relationship between its meaning and the state of the world is a matter of observation: it is either true of the world as it is, or not[18]. With historical text, on the other hand, observation is not an option. There is consequently no obvious way to determine its truth value, and thus no obvious way of deciding whether or not it is historically reliable, that is,

---

[16] Recent work with particular reference to historiography is Tully 1988; de Jackson 1989; Birch 1989; Gossman 1990

[17] Two recent exceptions are Mytum 1992 and Richter 1994

[18] This is the fundamental idea of truth-conditional semantics applied to natural language, for which see Partee *et al* 1990 and Cann1993

whether or not it accurately describes some state of the world in the past. There are two broad approaches to this problem.

The first is source criticism, which attempts to establish the probability of a text's historical reliability on, generally, four axes.

- Textual integrity: How sure can one be that the text in question is as its author intended it to be? Have there been additions or deletions of material, or changes of other sorts?

- Date: Ideally, a text should be contemporary with the things it describes. With one proviso, the general view is that the further a text is from contemporaneity, the less one should rely on it. The proviso is that later texts can, and demonstrably often do, incorporate earlier material. Source criticism is therefore much concerned with textual dating and with identification of chronological strata.

- Authoritativeness: Given parity of date, some texts are more authoritative than others, for a wide variety of reasons. A writer might, for example, have been particularly well placed in relation to the events he describes, or known to have been a careful (or careless) recorder; a text might be associated with a group of documents of established reliability, or be of a character which gives it some particular authority, such as annals in the chronological ordering of events.

- Bias There is no such thing as objective observation or description, since each of us interprets the world in accordance with our temperaments and experience. Over and above this, moreover, authors often consciously reinterpret their material in line with personal convictions and purposes. The aim is therefore to detect conscious or unconscious bias in particular authors and in groups or genres or text, so that due allowance can be made.

Source criticism is not uniformly effective, especially for documents as temporally remote as the ones used in this study. Editorial method is rigorous, but crucially dependent on the chance survival of textual recensions; dating criteria vary from absolutely secure through reasonably certain to nonexistent; criteria for authoritativeness may or may not be available; the determination of bias is most often a subjective thing, and as theories of source authors' motivations have become increasingly complex, so have they become increasingly fragile[19].

The second way of deciding on the reliability of historical texts, corroborative method, is orthogonal to source criticism. Consider this example. A murder has been committed in a London suburb in the early hours of Sunday morning. After a careful search the police identify three witnesses: a very aged woman who, unable to sleep, had been looking out onto the street when the murder happened, a drug dealer going home after a night's business, and a taxi driver who had dropped someone in the area shortly before. None of the witnesses knew one another prior to the event, and they did not communicate afterwards. They are, moreover, all of questionable reliability. The woman has poor eyesight, and admits to dozing occasionally. The dealer has little reason to cooperate with the police. The taxi driver caught only a brief glimpse as he drove by. Nevertheless, their statements to the police all agree that they saw a white male who had long hair, wore a leather jacket and jeans, dropped something into a sewer, and ran into the closest of the nearby tower blocks. Despite each individual's questionable reliability, the police inspector is rightly confident that this much, at least, of a suspect's description is true. Why? Because of the improbability of observers independently generating accounts which coincide to

---

[19] For example, the exquisitely complex and erudite analyses of Jordanes, Gregory of Tours, Paul the Deacon, and Bede in Goffart 1988

any significant degree. A rough quantification will show what is involved. This hypothetical description contains the following variables; in each case the probability of any one out of the total number of possibilities being randomly chosen (assuming equal probability) is attached[20]:

a) sex: male or female. 2 possibilities; prob: 0.50

b) race: white, black, Asian. 3 possibilities; prob: 0.33

c) hair style: estimate 6 possibilities; prob: 0.17

d) clothing: estimate 12 possibilities; prob: 0.08

e) dropped something: yes or no. 2 possibilities; prob: 0.50

f) where dropped: estimate 12 possibilities; prob: 0.08

g) escaped to: estimate 12 possibilities; prob: 0.08

Variables (a) - (g) are (i) not mutually exclusive and (ii) independent. By the standard rule for joint probabilities of independent events, the probability of one particular combination of variable values being randomly chosen out of all possible combinations of variable values is the product of the probabilities attached to (a) - (g), which is 0.00000718, or 7.18×10^{-6}. The chance of three identical independent random choices occurring is 0.00000718 x 0.00000718 x 0.00000718 $= 3.70 \times 10^{-16}$. The chance of three people independently guessing the same combination is therefore vanishingly small, and though such a coincidence is theoretically possible, for practical purposes one must assume that the old lady, the drug dealer, and the taxi driver agreed in their descriptions because they all witnessed the same reality.

The application to historical documents is self evident. If some number of them --the more the better-- agree in a significant set of features with respect to an object of interest, then those features can be taken as very likely to be historically true of that object, with the proviso that the documents must be genuinely

---

[20] For what follows see any textbook on probability theory, ie, Pitman 1993

independent. If there is any doubt, then confidence in the object's historicity is proportional to the conviction with which the documents' independence can be argued.

This study makes maximum possible use of the results of source criticism. With regard to some of the documentation used, in particular the Graeco-Roman and some of the early medieval Latin material, much has been demonstrated or convincingly argued, and it would be foolish to ignore these results despite the potential drawbacks mentioned earlier. On the other hand, intensive study of Anglo-Saxon vernacular poetry over many decades has yielded relatively little of use to the historian, and source criticism has thus far had only a limited application to most of the relevant Irish vernacular material; the study will make extensive use of both. That being so, the present discussion stakes its success on corroborative method, and its structure reflects this.

It has already been noted that the available documentation is widely distributed over time and space and that it occurs in clusters. Each cluster refers to some particular population group over some chronological span. The plan is to consider each of these clusters in isolation, abstracting whatever relevant information is offered, and using whichever source-critical results are available to assess that information's intrinsic credibility. Once all clusters have been studied independently in this way, corroborative method is applied to the results to determine the extent of agreement among them.

The evidence for the Celts and the Germans is examined in separate sections. This is done for convenience of exposition only. In particular, the discussion in no way depends on any assertion of ethnic uniformity either over time or place for either group, such as the older historiography tended to assume. There is substantial and undeniable empirical evidence for shared ethnic features, either by virtue of these linguistic groups having developed from a common cultural core, or been in prolonged contact with one another, or simply because primitive cultures tend to have certain characteristics. It is, however, also the case that the Irish Celts had a very different historical experience from the Gaulish ones, and the Goths from the Anglo-Saxons. To choose some cultural artefact from some Germanic or Celtic group, and to generalise it to all Germans or Celts, is a risky business, and this discussion makes no attempt to do so[21].

For clarity, a uniform structure is imposed on all the sections dealing with individual Germanic and Celtic groups. For each group, that structure is as follows:

- A brief historical introduction to provide a context for the discussion.
- A short account of the relevant features or lordship.
- The evidence for the cultivation of historical tradition. Any general observations that need to be made about the nature of the evidence are included here.
- The evidence for the interaction of lordship and historical tradition

---

[21] On this issue see Goffart 1980, especially the chapter 'The Germans. Historical Overview'

2. THE GERMANS

Historical overview

'Germans' is here used not in a political or even an ethnic sense, but simply to designate those barbarian European peoples who spoke one particular dialect of Indo-European, or who were dominated by Germanic-speaking lords[22]. If this specification seems pedantic or at least less helpful than it might be, it is only so because, when speaking of the early Germans, one has to be very careful. Nineteenth-century romanticism developed a view of a glorious, unified proto-Germanic culture, a *Germanentum*, which was given a philosphical basis of sorts toward the end of that century, political application in the twenties and thirties of this one, and, even now, after half a century of soul searching by Germans (in the political sense) young and old, is still the skeleton in the closet of attempts at European unification. The historical foundation of that *Germanentum* is long discredited[23], but as recently as 1980 William Goffart felt it necessary to devote a substantial part of an excellent book to a spirited, even vehement, refutation of the concept and of its application in historiography[24]. Goffart's suggestion that the early Germans be regarded as 'a collection of peoples who need have had no more in common than the mediterranean perspective in which they were seen'[25] has some rhetorical overstatement about it, but the point is taken.

The origins of the Germanic peoples are difficult if not impossible to reconstruct[26], and have as a topic had a fraught history intermingled with nationalism, as just noted. The mapping between archaeologically-based and linguistically Germanic groupings is more complicated than was supposed by the older scholarship, and documentary evidence for the earliest period is very sparse.

---

[22] On what is meant by a Germanic people see James 1988

[23] For example Graus 1965; Todd 1987, ch.1; Musset 1975 ch.1; Kruger 1983, chs. 1, 2

[24] Goffart 1980; also Goffart 1988

[25] Goffart 1980, 29

[26] For what follows see Musset 1975; Todd 1987; Kruger 1983; Wolfram 1990; Wolfram 1995

From what survives of his account, we know that, in the later fourth century BC, the navigator Pytheas of Marseilles sailed along the northern European shore as far, possibly, as the Elbe, and there found Gutones and Teutones --both Germanic names that were to resurface centuries later; according to Polybius Bastarnae and Skirians, who again are identified in later sources as Germans, were on the Black Sea at the end of the third century BC; between 113 and 101 BC Cimbri and Teutones were on the loose in Noricum, Italy, southern Gaul, and even Spain; the Greek ethnographer Posidonius (c.135 - 51 BC) used the name 'Germans' for the first time in distinguishing them from the Celts, but said no more about them.

These are scraps. The first substantial documentary evidence about the Germanic peoples is coterminous with the extension of Roman control north of the Alps in the mid-first century BC. Caesar's view of the situation at that time was straightforward: Gaulish territory was to the west of the Rhine, and Germanic territory to the east. The current general view is that Caesar drew this sharp demarcation for his own political ends, and that the situation was a good deal more complicated than he makes out. He himself says that the Treveri and Belgi to the north were of Germanic origin, and that groups of Germans were settled on the west bank of the Rhine; indeed, he had to fight off Ariovistus, leader of a confederate army whose aim was settlement in Gaul. Caesar risked an adventure to the east of the Rhine which, in terms of extension of Roman control, had no lasting effect. So, in 38 BC, did Agrippa, with the same result. In 12 BC Drusus, stepson of the emperor Augustus, began a German campaign which, under Tiberius, managed to secure large areas of the Germanic territory until 9 AD, when Arminius, a Cheruscan aristocrat and ex-Roman cavalry officer, led a revolt which virtually wiped out the Roman gains of the previous two decades. After Augustus' death in 14 AD his successor Tiberius began a reconquest and then abruptly aborted it two years later, apparently having decided that the German war had gone on long enough. Tiberius established a *limes* along the Rhine and the Danube which, consolidated by Vespasian and Domitian in the second half of the century, was to mark the boundary between the Empire and the Germanic peoples for almost three hundred years. The boundary was heavily fortified and needed to be, for border raiding by the Germans was endemic, and there were periodic large-scale inroads. In the mid-second century, for example, the Marcomanni managed to penetrate into northern Italy; in 254 AD the *limes* in upper Germany was breached, and between 268 and 278 AD there was barbarian raiding thoughout Gaul and even as far away as Spain; the Alemanni invaded Italy in 260 AD and again in 270 AD, and from 258 AD the Goths moved into Thrace, Greece, and Asia Minor. In all cases Rome reasserted itself, and by the end of the third century Diocletian had managed to restore order. But the fourth century saw the rise of larger, supra-tribal confederations and, by the end of the century, these federate peoples were to initiate migrations into western imperial territory --the famous *Völkerwanderungen*-- which, in the fifth and sixth, became full-scale settlements that formed the basis of the Germanic kingdoms of dark-age Europe: Ostrogoths and, later, Lombards in Italy, Burgundians and Franks in Gaul, Visigoths in Spain, Angles and Saxons in Britain.

a) THE EARLIEST GERMANS

The preceding historical overview noted that Caesar's *Gallic War* offers the first substantial insight into Germanic institutions. In the century and a half of war and commercial intercourse which followed, the Romans came to know more of their neighbours, and more accounts of the Germans begin to appear: in Strabo, writing early in the first century AD; in Pliny the Elder, who worked in the latter part of that century, and above all in Tacitus' *Germania* and *Annales*. We are concerned only with Tacitus.

i. Lordship among the early Germans[27]

Our primary source for lordship among the Germanic population groups of the first century AD is the *Germania*. Tacitus generalises his account over all these groups, and while the discussion has committed itself to the view that assumption of cultural uniformity at any given time is untenable, the position is that, in this case, there is no choice.

In a famous passage[28], Tacitus distinguishes two kinds of lord: *reges* and *duces*. The *rex*, 'king', is characterised by *nobilitas* --to a Roman, that meant aristocratic birth-- and a *dux*, 'leader', by *virtus*, 'valour'. This distinction has generated a good deal of scholarly debate, but ultimately it seems a functional rather than an institutional one. The *rex*, of royal blood, could be a battle leader when occasion demanded The *dux*, conversely, could if he was successful enough in war to establish his own domain take the title of *rex* and emerge as the founder of a *stirps regia*, a royal lineage. Both kinds of lord were crucially dependent on the *comitatus*, the retinue of warriors to whom the lord was bound by reciprocal oaths: he to lead and maintain them, they to commit themselves totally to his cause, even to the death. In peacetime, the size and 'keenness' of a retinue were what gave the lord status among his own and neighboring peoples. In war, these

---

[27] Wallace-Hadrill 1971, ch. 1, Hoops 1973, 'Adel' and 'Dux'; Kruger 1983, chs. VIII and XII; James 1988

[28] Much 1967, chs. 7 - 15, with associated commentary

same factors could bring victory. To recruit and maintain such a retinue, the lord had to gain a reputation as a man who was successful, that is, victorious in battle by virtue of his leadership and personal bravery, and moreover as a man who was generous, who would reward his men lavishly for their service. Since the wherewithal for generosity was the spoils of battle, it is clear that the engine of Tacitean Germanic lordship was war, and the aristocracy which exercised that lorship was a warrior aristocracy.

Some more or less contemporary examples put flesh on the bare bones of Tacitus' account[29]. One is Ariovistus, the Germanic leader whom Caesar encountered in the course of his subjugation of Gaul. Ariovistus led a confederation of disparate Germanic groups on a campaign of land conquest in the Gaulish territories bordering the Rhine. His position was such that Caesar saw fit to call him *rex Germanorum* and Pliny *rex Sueborum,* though it is not clear what his own followers regarded him as such, and we know nothing of his ancestry -- royal, noble, or otherwise. We do know that he was a successful battle leader, and that he exercised a power which Rome regarded as kingly. Marobodus, whom Tacitus calls *rex* of the Suebi and who is described as having *imperium,* 'ultimate authority' and *vis regia,* 'royal power', like Ariovistus commanded a confederation of disparate groups which he led into battle. He was *de genere nobilis,* 'of noble blood', and either belonged to or succeeded in establishing a *stirps regia,* 'royal lineage', among the Marcomanni. A third and final example is Arminius, the man who defeated Marobodus. He belonged to a *stirps regia,* and for twelve years led a large confederation not of disparate groups like Ariovistus and Marobodus but of whole peoples, without ever taking the title of *rex.* When he eventually tried to take that title, he was assassinated by relatives resentful of his arrogation of power. All three examples have elements of Tacitus' account of Germanic lorship, but at the same time make clear that that account is an abstraction of an untidy reality, not a statement of Germanic constitutional norms.

---

[29] What follows depends on Wallace-Hadrill 1971, 5 - 7

ii. Early Germanic historical tradition

The *Germania*

Why Tacitus wrote the *Germania* is not clear[30]. Some argue that he wanted to contrast the primitive virtues of the German barbarians with the decadence of his own countrymen for the latter's edification, others that he felt he had to alert Rome to the Germanic threat. There are problems with both; for present purposes, it doesn't really matter. What we do know is that he wrote in a well-established Graeco-Roman tradition of ethnography which had a structure and style all its own, and to which roughly the first half of the *Germania* adheres. A standard part of this ethnographical tradition was an account of the origins of the people in question. On that subject, Tacitus includes the following well known passage[31]:

> *They celebrate in ancient songs, which is the only sort of memorial and historical record they have, Tuisto, a god born of the earth. To him they attribute a son Mannus the beginning and founder of the race ('gens'), and to Mannus three sons, from whose names those near the ocean are called Ingaevones, those in the middle Herminones, and the rest Istaevones. Some, using the licence of antiquity, declare for more sons born to the god and more tribal names - Marsi, Suebi, Gambrivii, Vandilii - and that these are true and ancient names.*

This passage shows (i) that the cultivation of orally-transmitted song was sufficiently widespread among at least some Germanic peoples of the first century AD --which ones precisely is not clear-- for Tacitus to identify it as a cultural characteristic, (ii) that, even then, it was a long-established institution among them, (iii) that the function of this institution was to preserve history, though one

---

[30] Martin 1981, 49-58; see also the excellent brief assessment in Wallace-Hadrill 1971, ch. 1

[31] There is a large literature on this passage. See primarily Hauck 1955 and 1964; Wenskus 1961; Much 1967, 44 and associated commentary.; Höfler 1973

is here obviously dealing with mythological tradition rather than historical tradition in the modern sense, and (iv) that 'history' included an origin legend which drew the descent of certain Germanic groups from a god.

The *Germania* also says that *they remember that Hercules had been among them, and sing about him as the foremost among strong men in battle.* Hercules is an *interpretatio Romana* of a Germanic god[32]; as in the preceding passage, Tacitus here claims that the Germans to whom he was referring maintained orally-transmitted historical / mythological tradition.

The *Annales*

The *Annales* end their account of the Germanic leader Arminius as follows[33]:

He completed thirty seven years of life, including twelve of power, and to this day is sung about among the barbarian peoples.

Arminius[34] has already been referred to in the preceding discussion. He was a nobleman among the Cherusci who had served as an officer in the Roman auxiliary army and even become a Roman citizen. When, in 9 AD, Publius Quintilius Varus led an army into Cheruscan territory, Arminius countered with a tribal alliance and inflicted a famous deafeat on him in the Teutoburger Wald. In 16 AD he managed to survive another Roman attack, shortly after which Tiberius called off the German war and began the establishment of the *limes,* leaving the Germanic tribes to the east of the Rhine free of Roman domination. Thereafter, according to Tacitus, Arminius' desire for kingship led to tensions with the Cheruscan aristocracy, and in 21 AD he was assassinated by kinsmen.

---

[32] Much 1967 74 ff

[33] Koestermann 1965, II.88

[34] Arminius was and to some extent still is a hero in Germany, and references to him both in scholarly and in popular literature are very numerous. Good modern accounts are Hoops 1973, 'Arminius' and Kruger 1983, 281 ff

Arminius was a major figure in the political life of his people, and more broadly for the tribal coalition which he led. Several generations later, when Tacitus wrote, there were songs about him, though what these songs were about is not clear. A reasonable assumption would be that his was not an isolated case, and that songs about other great leaders also existed. Tacitus' Germans therefore maintained orally transmitted traditions not only about gods but also about important leaders.

iii. Lordship and historical tradition among the early Germans

What can the motivation for drawing the descent of population groups from a god have been? The answer emerges from an account in the second part of the *Germania,* which, instead of the ethnographical generalisations of the first part, concentrates on accounts of individual Germanic tribes. It describes a religious ceremony which the Suebi, one of the tribes mentioned in the alternative version of the genealogy which Tacitus appends to his Mannus narrative, celebrated in the territory of one of its constituent subgroups, the Semnones[35]. *The Semnones traditionally maintain that they are the most ancient and most noble of the Suebi,* writes Tacitus, adding, *This belief in their antiquity is confirmed by their religion.* In the ceremony which is then described, *all the peoples of the same blood* meet in a forest in the Semnones' territory and there offer a human sacrifice; Tacitus explains the significance of it all:

> *The whole superstition looks back to this: it is as if the tribe* ('gens') *began there, as if the god who is ruler of all were there, and everything else is subject and obedient to him. The prosperity of the Semnones adds to their authority. A hundred districts are inhabited by them, and because of this great number they believe themselves to be chief of the Suebi.*

---

[35] Much 1967, 432 with associated commentary

The Suebi were a large and powerful confederation of Germanic groups as early as the first century BC[36]. To establish their ethnic unity they had a myth of common descent from a god, which its cultic enactment was intended to demonstrate[37]. This myth was, moreover, exploited for political ends within the confederation. The Semnones were a dominant subgroup among the Suebi, and legitimised their *de facto* dominance by exploiting the myth of common descent in that they claimed a special proximity to the divine progenitor of the tribe to which they belonged.

Given that the element of divine descent is common to this account and to the Mannus genealogy, it seems reasonable to suppose that the mythology underlying the Suebic cult was articulated in *ancient songs*. Two considerations support this. The first is textual. The Latin text says of the cult that *vetustissimos nobilissimosque Sueborum Semnones* **memorant**, 'The Semnones traditionally maintain that they are the most ancient and most noble of the Suebi'; the Mannus passage says: *celebrant carminibus antiquis, quod unum apud illos* **memoriae et** *annalium genus est*, 'They celebrate in ancient songs, which is the only sort of memorial and historical record they have'; and the Hercules passage reads: *Fuisse apud eos et Herculem* **memorant**, 'they remember that Hercules had been among them'. The notion of remembrance in the latter two passages refers explicitly to songs, which indicates that it does in the first as well. The other consideration is that the Suebi are actually mentioned in the alternative version of the Mannus genealogy, thus providing an explicit link between it and the account of the Semnones. If these arguments are accepted, then the conclusion is that, among Tacitus' Germans, orally transmitted song was the vehicle for mythological-historical tradition which served to consolidate ethnic consciousness and legitimise political authority.

---

[36] On the Suebi see Kruger 1983, 222-5

[37] For detailed commentaries on this observation see Wenskus 1961, 234 ff; Hauck 1955, 1964; Höfler (1973)

b) THE GOTHS[38]

Whether or not the Goths originally came from Scandinavia as their own traditions claimed has long been disputed[39], but in the first century AD *Gutones* (Pliny, c.75 AD) and *Gothones* (Tacitus, 98 AD) were in north-eastern Germany, and a little later Ptolemy places them on the lower Vistula[40]. By the early third century they were settled in an area to the north and west of the Black Sea. In 238 AD they began raiding Imperial territory --the shores of the Black Sea, Thrace, and even beyond the Bosphorus; for about a century Gothic-occupied territory bordered the Roman Empire along and to the north of the Danube from Pannonia to the Black Sea. It was during this time that the Goths split into two groups[41] which retained their identities for many centuries, the Terwingi and the Greutingi, or, as they came to be known later, the Visigoths and the Ostrogoths. In 375 AD began the incursion of the Huns which fragmented what until then had been an increasingly stable Gothic society, and caused migrations which were to take the Visigoths to Spain and the Ostrogoths into Italy.

The Visigoths moved south-westerwards over the Danube. One group, led by Fritigern, demanded and got asylum within the Empire, and was settled in Dacia. The other, under Athanaric, accepted the overlordship of the Huns and settled in the region of present-day Moldavia. The Dacian Goths quickly began to cause trouble, and even besieged the Imperial city of Constantinople, but in 401 AD Alaric suddenly decided to lead his people into Italy. For several years they were at large in northern and central Italy, and in 410 AD sacked Rome itself. From there they headed south intending to cross into Africa, but were unsuccessful and, under Alaric's successor Athaulf, went northwards and arrived in Gaul by 412 AD, where they took Narbonne, Toulouse, and Bordeaux. This was the basis of the kingdom of Toulouse, which was to last until the turn of the

---

[38] Wolfram 1980; also Wenskus 1961, 462 ff
[39] Wolfram 1980, 6 ff and 32 ff; also Goffart 1988, 30 ff and 87 ff
[40] Wolfram 1980, 5 ff and 32 ff
[41] Wolfram 1980, 13 ff

century, when pressure from the Franks resulted in a mass Visigothic exodus into northern Spain. There they established the kingdom of Toledo, which came to an end with the Islamic invasion of 711 AD.

The Ostrogoths had settled in Pannonia on the middle Danube as subjects of the Huns and, indeed, fought alongside Attila in his wars. When Attila died in 454 AD, the Ostrogothic leader Valamir agreed a *foedus* with the Empire which was sporadically observed until, under Valamir's son Theodoric, the Ostrogoths began a migration which took them, between 475 and 488 AD, to Moesia, Macedonia, Dacia, and Constantinople. In Constantinople Theodoric reached an agreement with the emperor Zeno to drive Odoacer out of Italy, and began the task in 489 AD; by 493 it was complete, and Theodoric declared himself king of Italy, a status confirmed in 497 AD by the emperor Anastasius. Theodoric had in his youth spent time as a hostage in Constantinople, and was well placed to deal sympathetically and competently with the Roman administrative and social structures which were in place. His policy was rigidly to separate Romans and Ostrogoths in all spheres of life, and this worked well for almost the whole of his rule. Theodoric died in 526 AD and power was transferred smoothly to his son Athalaric, but when Athalaric died without an heir in 534 AD there was a period of intrigue followed by an attempt by the eastern emperor Justinian to reconquer Italy for the Empire. The Romano-Gothic kingdom collapsed, and for a quarter century the war continued. Italy was devastated, and the Ostrogoths disappeared from history as a recognisable ethnic entity.

i. Gothic Lordship[42]

During the fourth century the Greutingi fade out of the Imperial consciousness, and thereby of history, but information about the Terwingi becomes plentiful enough to be able to construct a coherent picture of lordship among them at that time. In 'normal' times, that is, when not at war or migrating,

---

[42] Wolfram 1970; 1975a; 1975b; 1975c; 1980

the *kuni is* the primary political unit, where *kuni* means what its etymology says it should: an *Abstammungsgemeinschaft,* a group which perceived itself as sharing common descent. At its head was a *reiks* drawn from a landed aristocracy, the leader of the *harjis* or assembled military resources of the *kuni.* The individual aristocrat was the *frauja* at the head of an extended family, with a house or *gards* on which the family was centred, and a retinue warriors *(andbahtos, siponeis).* How precisely one *frauja* became a *reiks* of the *kuni* rather than another is not clear, but it is reasonable to suppose, guided by Tacitus, that relative status and power measured by wealth and size of retinue were crucial. In 'abnormal' times, individual *kuni* would draw together for mutual support and appoint, again in some unspecified way, a 'judge' *(iudex)* to lead the *gutthiuda,* the 'Gothic people' consisting of Terwingi and associated groups such as the Taifals.

By the early fifth century, the Goths of the kingdom of Toulouse had a royal family, the Balts, from which successive kings came[43]. So, in Theodoric's kingdom of Italy, did the Ostrogoths: the Amals[44]. In the case of the Visigoths there had been a development from the rather distributed Terwing lordship described above, with a 'constitutional' --and temporary-- non-royal monarch governing in principle independent *reiks*-lordships, to a centralised monarchy controlled by a single family. How this happened is not clear. It was probably a response to the special circumstances of the mass migration which the Visigoths undertook in the late fourth and early fifth centuries[45]. For present purposes, however, it is more important to note the development than to discover its causes. As regards the Ostrogoths, no development needs to be explained, since we lack a correspondingly detailed account of earlier Greuting lordship.

---

[43] Wolfram 1980, 246 ff
[44] Wolfram 1980, 353 ff
[45] Wolfram 1980, 169-74

ii. Gothic historical tradition

The *Getica*[46] is the main source of evidence for historical tradition among the Goths. It was written in Constantinople by the Goth Jordanes in 551 AD or shortly thereafter. Jordanes himself says in his preface that he based it on a Gothic history written by Cassiodorus, the chief minister of Theodoric in Italy, sometime between 519 and 533 AD. Cassiodorus' work is now lost, and it is consequently impossible to say with any certainty what Jordanes did with his source, though the likelihood is that it is a fairly free abridgment. Jordanes moreover says that he used various other sources, and so one cannot in general even be sure what does and what does not derive from Cassiodorus. Nor is Jordanes' motivation for writing at all clear. By the mid-sixth century Justinian had just finished destroying the Ostrogothic kingdom in Italy, and to compose a book in the Imperial capitol extolling the Goths in general and the Amal dynasty which had ruled that kingdom in particular seems inappropriate to say the least. That Cassiodorus' text should come to us through a filter with largely imponderable properties is especially unfortunate because Cassiodrous was by virtue of his position uniquely placed to observe the Ostrogoths at first hand.

Jordanes, or much more likely his source Cassiodorus, drew on historical tradition in reconstructing Gothic history[47]. This is clear from explicit references to vernacular material at various points in the *Getica,* but there are also occasional passages where stylistic features point to such a source. In the latter case there is an inevitable element of subjectivity, and one is well advised to heed Andreas Heusler's advice, given long ago[48] that *wo es in den Chroniken lebhaft und dramatisch zugeht, darf man nicht gleich mit der Liedquelle kommen,* 'where things get exciting and dramatic in the historical documents, one must not immediately invoke a source in oral tradition'. Excessive scepticism is also a

---

[46] Mommsen 1882; the account which follows depends on the detailed discussion of the *Getica* and its sources together with extensive references to earlier work in Goffart 1988, ch.2. On Cassiodorus' methods and orientation see further Wolfram 1981 and O'Donnell 1979
[47] But see Goffart's 1988 views on this in the discussion to follow
[48] Heusler 1923, 147

danger, but, to forestall criticism, such passages are used only in a supporting role for the explicit vernacular source citations.

Jordanes begins the *Getica* with an account of the very early history of the Goths[49]. It commences with the departure from their northern homeland[50]: *From this island of Scandia...the Goths are said to have come long ago with their king Berig.* After a period of settlement Filimer, the fifth king since Berig, led his people to Scythia and then to Pontus, *as is generally rehearsed in their ancient songs in almost historical fashion*[51]. Later in the *Getica* Jordanes again has occasion to refer to Filimer when writing of the Huns[52]: *For, as antiquity reports, we have heard that they came into being as follows* --Filimer banished certain witches who, raped by demons, gave birth to the Huns. Given that Gothic *ancient songs* existed about Filimer, the meaning of *antiquity* in the latter passage seems clear. Also attached to this section on the earliest history of the Goths is the comment[53]:

> *Nor do we find anywhere in their written records legends which tell of their subjection to slavery in Britain or in some other island, or of their redemption by a certain man at the cost of a single horse. Of course, if anyone in our city says that the Goths had an origin different from the one I have related, let him object. For myself, I prefer to believe what I have read rather than put trust in old wives' tales.*

Having brought the Goths as far as the Black Sea, Jordanes divides the Goths into two branches, the Visigoths and the Ostrogoths. Thereupon comes the observation[54]: *In earliest times they sang the deeds of their ancestors in strains of song accompanied by the cithara, chanting of Eterpamara, Hanala, Fritigern,*

---

[49] On the following references see Richter 1994, 156 ff
[50] Mommsen 1882, 60
[51] Mommsen 1882, 61
[52] Mommsen 1882, 89
[53] Mommsen 1882, 63
[54] Mommsen 1882, 65

Vidigoia, and others whose fame among them is great, such heroes as admiring antiquity scarce proclaims its own to be. Of these at least one, Fritigern, is known to have been historical: he led the Terwingi into Roman territory in response to the Hunnish attack in 375 AD, and it was under him that the Goths won their famous victory against the Romans at Adrianople in 378 AD[55].

After some intervening material irrelevant to present concerns, Jordanes locates the Goths in Dacia and recounts a great victory which they gained over the Romans[56]:

> *And because of the great victory they had won in this region, they thereafter called their leaders, by whose good fortune they seemed to have conquered, not mere men but demigods, that is, ansis. I will briefly run through their genealogy, telling the lineage of each and the beginning and end of this line...Now the first of these heroes, as they themselves relate in their legends, was Gapt, who begat Hulmul. And Hulmul begat Augis, and Augis begat him who was called Amal, from whom the name of the Amali comes. This Amal begat Hisarnis, and Hisarnis begat Ostrogotha...*

The genealogy goes on at some length in this vein, and soon gets away from mythical and legendary figures like those included in the above quotation and onto persons known from various other sources to have been historical; it ends with Athalaric, the grandson of Theodoric the Great.

At a later stage in the *Getica*, Jordanes describes the histories of the Visigoths and the Ostrogoths separately. There is one passage of interest in each of these sections. The Visigothic one is about Theodorid, who was killed fighting alongside the Romans against Attila[57]:

> *The Visigoths sought their king, and the king's sons their father...*

---

[55] Wolfram 1980, 79-81 and 137-153
[56] Mommsen 1882, 76. This passage has a large associated literature: see Moisl 1979; Wolfram 1977 and 1980, 23 ff; Goffart 1988 ch.2
[57] Mommsen 1882, 112-13

When, after a long search, they found him where the dead lay
thickest, as happens with brave men, they honoured him with songs
and bore him away in the sight of the enemy. You might have seen
bands of Goths fighting with dissonant cries and paying honour to
the dead while the battle still raged.

This passage is interesting from two points of view. Obvious is the practice of singing songs about a fallen king. Less so is the observation that it in certain respects resembles extant *Heldensage*-type texts, with the implication that this story about Theodorid comes, like *Heldensage*, from an orally transmitted vernacular source --the treatment of the fallen hero in the Old English *Dream of the Rood*[58] for example, and Beowulf's funeral in the poem of that name[59]. The Ostrogothic passage has to do with Thorismund, son of Ermanaric[60]:

In the second year of his rule he moved an army against the Gepidae
and won a great victory over them, but is said to have been killed by
falling from his horse. When he was dead, the Ostrogoths mourned
for him so deeply that for forty years no other king succeeded him,
and during all this time they had ever on their lips the tale of his
memory.

The interest of this passage is that great kings are remembered over long periods, its full significance emerges when seen in conjunction with the above-quoted passage about Fritigern and Vidigoia.

It can on the basis of this survey be said that the maintenance of traditions relating to tribal history was an established institution among the Goths at least until the time of Cassiodorus / Jordanes. This body of tradition included the tribal origin legend, accounts of the careers of prominent leaders of the past, and, among the Ostrogoths, a royal dynastic history which drew the descent of the

---

[58] Swanton 1970, lines 60-77
[59] Klaeber 1951, lines 3156-3182
[60] Mommsen 1882, 122

Amals from deified heroes; in some cases at least, such traditions were in the form of song.

The existence of such Gothic tradition is corroborated by the occurence of Gothic characters in medieval *Heldensage*. For example, Fritigern, Vidigoia, and possibly Eterpamara occur as the Fridga, Wudga, and --less certainly-- Emerca which are mentioned as Gothic kings in the Old English poem *Widsith*[61]. *Widsith's* Eastgota and his son Unwen correspond to Ostrogotha, sixth in descent in the *Getica's* Amal genealogy, and to Ostrogotha's son Hunuil[62]. Ermanaric and Theodoric, moreover, are among the most famous figures of Germanic *Heldensage*[63], and are variously attested in, among others, the Old English poems *Widsith, Deor, Waldere,* and *Beowulf;* Jordanes' account of Ermanarich's killing of Sunhilda occurs also in the thirteenth-century Scandinavian *Hamðismal*[64].

iii. Lordship and historical tradition among the Goths

The argument that historical tradition was used to legitimise Gothic lordship centres on the Amal genealogy cited above. Cassiodorus compiled the genealogy for Athalaric. We know this from a letter sent by Athalaric to the Roman Senate, but actually drafted by Cassiodorus, which says that *Cassiodorus extended his labours even to our remote ancestry...He restored the Amals to their proper place in all the lustre of their lineage, proving indubitably that for 17 generations we had kings for our ancestors...*[65]. This was part of Cassiodorus' larger mission of making the new Gothic masters acceptable to their senatorial subjects --to show that, like the senators themselves, the Amals had a long and distinguished ancestry; indeed, there were 17 generations from Gapt to Athalaric as there were 17 from Aeneas to Romulus in Roman tradition, the implication

---

[61] Malone 1962, lines 151, 212-13, 145-6

[62] Malone 1962, lines 142-3, 206. Hunuil also occurs as Unwine in Layamon's *Brut;* see Brook 1963

[63] Schneider 1962; Uecker 1972

[64] von See 1971, 61

[65] Mommsen 1894, IX 25, 4

being that Athalaric was the new Romulus[66]. We also know from Jordanes that at least the early stages of descent in the Amal genealogy were taken from Gothic orally-transmitted legends. The conclusion would, therefore, appear to be that Gothic historical tradition was used on Theodoric's behalf to legitimize his lordship. There is, however, a problem what must be dealt with before this conclusion can stand.

The problem has to do with a curious aberration in the otherwise excellent discussion of Jordanes' *Getica* and its background by Goffart 1988, which should be read in conjunction with Wolfram 1981. The aberration is this: though the *Getica* contains several explicit references to vernacular sources, Goffart seems intent on denying that such sources had an important role to play either in Cassiodorus' or in Jordanes' work. His argument proceeds in the following stages: (i) despite being in a uniquely advantageous position to observe and record Gothic instititions (1988, 28), Cassiodorus took little interest in vernacular traditions (1988, 35 ff, 86), and so (ii) the references to Gothic traditions are very probably attributable to Jordanes rather than to Cassiodorus (1988, 35ff, 76, 86), but (iii) Jordanes would, in mid-sixth century Constantinople, have been poorly placed for access to Gothic historical tradition (1988, 30), and consequently (iv) we can safely disregard the supposed vernacular component in the work of Cassiodorus / Jordanes, and more particularly as a source for the Amal genealogy.

All this is based on an observation which Casssiodorus makes on Athalaric's behalf in the above-mentioned letter: Cassiodorus *extended his labours even to our remote ancestry, discovering in books that which scarcely the hoar memories of our forefathers preserved. He drew forth from their hiding place the kings of the Goths, concealed by long forgetfulness...collecting into a single wreath the varied flowers that were formerly strewn here and there in fields of books.* Goffart himself admits that this is a shaky foundation --that 'it is not an author's precise and exhaustive description of his sources of information' (1988,

---

[66] Wolfram 1967, 99-103; Wolfram 1968; Wolfram 1980, 23 ff; Goffart 1988 ch.2; Wolfram

35). Interpretations other than his are not only possible but also more probable. Cassiodorus, a Roman aristocrat making a point about Amal descent to Roman aristocratic colleagues, would naturally want to validate that descent from the sort of source which those colleagues would have regarded as respectable: books. Those books may well have contained references to Gothic leaders which the putative Amal historical tradition did not include. After all, it would be an overwhelming coincidence if that tradition contained exactly the required 17 generations; Amal kings 'lost' from the historical tradition could therefore be 'found'. Moreover, the earliest stages of the genealogy contains an item of Germanic mythological vocabulary together with names which Cassiodorus would not have found in any of his books, and which must have come from Gothic traditional sources. The piece of mythological terminology is *ansis*, which Jordanes translates as *semidei*, and which corresponds, for example, to the *esa* (sg. *os*) who are named along with elves and witches in an Old English charm[67], and to the *aesir* (sg. *ass),* the gods of North Germanic mythology[68]. There is a large literature on Gapt, and it is almost certain that he corresponds to *Gautaz, a deity who appears in a variety of Germanic mythologies and is in some cases identified with Woden[69]. Hulmul corresponds to Humli, a god in later Danish mythology[70]. Another way of looking at the genesis of the Amal genealogy, then, is to see Cassiodorus supplementing the historical Amal tradition from Roman historical sources. This has the added advantage of being in accord with what Jordanes' text actually says.

Why Goffart is so hostile to historical tradition is not entirely clear. It does, however, appear to have something to do with the reliability of such tradition (1988, 30) -which, of course, is an issue orthogonal to present

---

1990, 52-59
[67] Whitelock 1967, 101
[68] Pokorny 1959 for these and other cognates; also Kuhn 1973
[69] Moisl 1979
[70] Wolfram 1977

concerns-- leading into the legend of the Gothic origin in Scandinavia (1988, 30), and thence to the grand theme of a common *Germanentum* which, throughout his book, he is rightly concerned to demolish. It remains, however, that Goffart's argument, discussed above, is far from compelling, and that a good case remains for the conclusion proposed earlier: that Gothic historical tradition was used on Theodoric's behalf to legitimize his lordship.

c) THE LOMBARDS[71]

The Lombards may or may not originally have come from Scandinavia[72] but we know from occasional contemporary references in Classical texts that, in the first and second centuries AD, they lived in the region of the lower Elbe. Thereafter they all but disappear from the historical record until the end of the fifth century, at which time they were settled in an area corresponding to present day Lower Austria. Not long afterwards they moved into Pannonia, where they remained until, in 568 AD, their king Alboin led them into Italy. By the end of the sixth century the entire northern part of the country was under their control, and they had begun to move southwards into Benevento and Umbria; this Lombard kingdom lasted until 774 AD, when it was annexed by Charlemagne.

i. Lombard lordship

The above-mentioned Classical references are brief and not very informative. For substantive information about Lombard institutions we depend on a few 7th-9th century texts[73]: the *Edict* issued by King Rothari in 643 AD, the *Origo Gentis Langobardorum* compiled sometime during Rothari's reign (636-52 AD), Paul the Deacon's later-eighth century *Historia Langobardorum*[74] and the *Historia Langobardorum codicis Gothani* written between 807 and 812 AD. On the basis of these sources, one can say that the foundation of the 'original' Lombard lordship --what they brought with them from Pannonia-- was the *fara,* a term whose precise meaning has been a matter of some debate[75] but which appears to denote a group centred on an aristocratic kindred, and led by a *dux* with a personal retinue or, in Tacitean terms, a *comitatus*. It was from such aristocratic families that Lombard kings were drawn. Certain of these families

---

[71] For the Lombards generally see Wenskus 1961, 485 ff; Kruger 1981, 584- 96; Jarnut 1981; Whickham 1981; Menghin 1985; Christie 1995
[72] Goffart 1988, 382 ff
[73] Menghin 1985, 8 ff
[74] On Paul the Deacon and his work see Goffart 1988
[75] On Lombard lordship see Hoops 1973, 'fara'; Barnwell 1997, ch.3

were, moreover, able to retain the kingship over consecutive reigns, and thereby to become royal dynasties. This emerges from the succession of kings which the *Origo* and Paul's *Historia* describe. Originally, says Paul, two *duces* Ibor and Agio jointly led the Lombards from their ancestral home, but, after their deaths *the Lombards, no longer wishing to be under duces, established a king for themselves like other peoples. Therefore Agelmund the son of Agio first reigned over them, drawing from his lineage the beginning of the Gungingi, which among them was considered very noble*[76]. Agelmund was succeeded by an adopted son Lamissio. The tenure of the Gungingi was followed by that of the Lethingi, who provided six kings, that of the Lethingi by the Gausi, who provided two, and the Gausi in their turn by the Beleos, also with two[77].

ii. **Lombard historical tradition**[78]

Both the compiler of the *Origo Gentis Langobardorum* and Paul the Deacon drew, directly or indirectly, on vernacular Lombard traditions in constructing their respective histories[79]. Indications that this was so are of two sorts: (i) explicit citation of oral sources in the narrative, and (ii) features of style and/or content which point to such sources. There is an element of subjectivity with (ii), as already noted with regard to Gothic tradition, but excessive scepticism is also a danger.

The *Origo* and the *Historia* both begin their accounts of Lombard history by telling how a group going by the name of Winnili departed Scandinavia under the leadership of the two *duces* Ibor and Agio mentioned above[80]. Early in their wanderings the Winnili are threatened by Vandals and, in desperation, they appeal to the goddess Frea to intercede with her husband Woden on their behalf. Woden grants them victory over the Vandals, and at the same time gives them a name by

---

[76] Waitz 1878, 1, 15-17
[77] See the genealogical table inside the back cover of Menghin 1985
[78] Gschwantler 1979 reviews most of the evidence
[79] On the close relationship of these texts see Gschwantler 1976
[80] Waitz 1878, 2-3 and 52-6 respectively

which they are subsequently to be known: Langobardi. The natural assumption must be that this story, with its element of pagan Germanic mythology, derives from Lombard historical tradition. This is directly confirmed in the text. Paul introduces his version of the departure from Scandinavia with *ut fertur*, 'as is reported'; the Woden story begins with the words *refert hoc loco antiquitas ridiculam fabulam*, 'antiquity here reports a ridiculous story', and ends: *Haec risui digna sunt et pro nihilo habenda*, 'these things are worthy of laughter and to be disregarded'. The *Historia Langobardorum codicis Gothani*, moreover, begins a rather different version of the story with *Asserunt antiqui parentes Langobardorum...*, 'the ancient fathers of the Lombards declare'[81]. We are, in fact, here dealing with the Lombard tribal origin legend, in which the Lombards traced their ethnic identity to the patronage of a god[82].

After the defeat of the Vandals, the *Origo* and the *Historia* take the Lombards further on their wanderings. The *Origo* at this point becomes little more than an annotated king-list. Paul, however, maintains a well-developed narrative, and, though he gives no explicit indication of vernacular sources, certain episodes have a character which strongly suggest an origin in the same body of tradition as the departure from Scandinavia and the Woden episode: how the Lombards managed to intimidate an enemy people by pretending to have among them especially terrifying warriors with dogs' heads; how they triumphed over the same people by arranging and winning a single combat between champions; how, in order to build up their numbers, they allowed captives to join them by taking a solemn oath.

Paul and the *Origo* then proceed to recount the creation of the first king, Agelmund. The *Historia* here includes a story of how Agelmund's eventual successor was born. A prostitute gave birth to seven sons and threw them into a pond to drown. Agelmund happened to ride by and prodded them with his spear,

---

[81] Waitz 1878, Hist. Lang. cod. Goth. 1
[82] Hauck 1955; Wenskus 1961, 485-88; Höfler 1973; Gschwantler 1979

whereupon one of them grabbed the spear. Agelmund pulled him out, named him Lamissio, and pronounced him his successor. The legendary character of the story is manifest, and there are indications of a mythical origin[83]; the implication of a vernacular source is confirmed by explicit indications that the *Origo* and the *Historia* both had access to traditions about Agelmund's reign. The *Origo* says *...et dicitur quia fecerunt sibi regem nomine Agelmund*, 'it is said that they made for themselves a king named Agelmund', and Paul, summing up his account of Agelmund's reign, writes *...sicut a maioribus traditur, tribus et triginta annis Langobardorum tenuit regnum*, 'as is transmitted to us by our ancestors, he held the kingship for thirty three years'. Paul also tells how Lamissio fought and won a single combat against a race of amazon-like women, and how he took revenge on the Bulgarians for killing his father[84]. The first is introduced by *ferunt*, 'they say', and the second has narrative features with close parallels in medieval *Heldensage* literature[85].

Our two texts now arrange Lombard history according to the reigns of successive kings. The order is the same in both, but, as noted, the *Origo is* little more than an annotated king-list, while the *Historia* goes into considerable narrative detail. The four kings who follow Lamissio --Lethu, Hildeoc, Gudeoc, and Claffo-- are as briefly documented in the *Historia* as in the *Origo*, and the only indication of a vernacular source comes from the latter with reference to Lethu: *...et dicitur quia regnasset annos plus minus quadraginta*, 'it is said that he ruled about forty years'. For the seventh king Tato, Paul's narrative is once again much fuller. It includes a story of how Tato's daughter had the brother of Rodolf, king of the Herules, murdered while he was at the Lombard court, and how this led to a war between the two peoples[86]; here again there are *Heldensage*-type features[87]. Waccho and Waltari are only briefly mentioned, but by way of

---

[83] Waitz 1878, 1, 15-17; Hauck 1955; Höfler 1973
[84] Waitz 1878 1, 15-17
[85] On the vernacular sources for Lamissio's reign see Gschwantler 1979, 60-61
[86] Waitz 1878, 1, 20
[87] Gschwantler 1979, 61-3

42

compensation the careers of Audoin and Alboin, who follow them, are very fully described. In fact, virtually everything that Paul says about Audoin comes from the *Turisindsage*[88] and for Alboin he includes the *Rosimundsage*[89], both of which are standardly treated in *Heldensage* scholarship as a vernacular Lombard heroic poems in Latin translation[90]. Paul furthermore attests the existence of an extensive body of historical tradition about Alboin in a well known passage[91]:

> *The glorious name of Alboin was spread far and wide to such an extent that even until now his generosity and glory, his success and strength in battles is celebrated both among the Bavarians and the Saxons, but also among other men speaking the same language, in their songs.*

The accounts of Alboin's successor Cleph and of the interregnum which followed him contain nothing of interest here. For Authari, however, there are two relevant episodes: a romantic story about the wooing of the Bavarian king's daughter Theudelinda[92], and a brief note[93], introduced by *about this time is supposed to have happened, what is recounted about King Authari. The story is this...,* which tells how the king rode to the southernmost part of Italy, *and because it was said that a certain column stood in the waves of the sea, he approached it astride his horse, and touching it with his spear said: 'The borders of the Lombards will reach to here'.* For Agilulf, Adaloald, and Arioald there is again nothing of interest. That brings us to Rothari; for reasons about to emerge, the survey can end here.

In view of what has been said, it is fair to conclude that a substantial body of vernacular Lombard historical tradition was available to ecclesiastical writers working between the seventh and ninth centuries, and that it described the origin

---

[88] Waitz 1878, 1, 22-4 and 27
[89] Waitz 1878, 2, 28-30
[90] Schneider 1962, vol. 2, 141-5; von See 1971, 74 ff.; Uecker 1972, 129-34; Gschwantler 1976 and 1979
[91] Waitz 1878, 1, 27
[92] Waitz 1878, 3, 30
[93] Waitz 1878, 3, 32

of the Lombards, their early history, and the careers of at least some of their kings up at least until the late sixth or early seventh century. The existence of such tradition can, as with the Goths, be corroborated from surviving early medieval *Heldensage:* the Old English poem *Widsith*[94] refers to Ælfwine (Alboin), Eadwine (Audoin), and Ægelmund.

ii. **Lordship and historical tradition among the Lombards**

King Rothari made the body of tradition presented in the preceding section the basis of political propaganda. His *Edict,* a collection of laws which he issued in 643 AD, is the key to showing this. The laws themselves are prefaced by an introduction in which Rothari first of all states his motivations --to help remedy the sad state of affairs of the kingdom, to alleviate oppression of the poor by the rich-- and then goes on[95]:

> *We have found it useful as a memorial for future times to*
> *command that the names of the kings of our ancestors ever*
> *since kings began to be named among our Lombard people,*
> *and in so far as we were able to learn them from old men, to*
> *be committed to writing in this book.*

There follows a list of Lombard kings extending from Agelmund to Rothari himself; to his own name he attaches a list of eleven ancestors in his family, the Harudi.

There are three main reasons for thinking that this list was intended by Rothari as political propaganda:

- It is generally recognised that, among the early Germanic peoples as in comparable societies elsewhere, genealogies and regnal lists are not primarily historical records but political instruments[96]; we have seen two examples --

---

[94] Malone 1962, lines 126-7 and 139; also Wenskus 1961, 489-90
[95] Pertz 1868, 386
[96] Wenskus 1976; Dumville 1977; Vansina 1985, 182 ff

Tacitus' Mannus genealogy and the Amal genealogy in Jordanes-- and will be looking at an Anglo-Saxon example later. When, therefore, Rothari is seen to publish a king-list which claims to itemise kings of the Lombards beginning with the first and ending with himself, and which includes his own genealogy, one is entitled at least to suspect that it was intended to be politically functional in some way.

- There are 17 kings, Rothari himself included, in the list. We have already looked at the significance of this apparently unremarkable number with regard to the Gothic Amal genealogy[97], where the 17 generations from Gapt to Athalaric were meant to parallel the 17 from Aeneas to Romulus in contemporary Roman tradition, a coincidence which Cassiodorus arranged to imply that Athalaric was the new Romulus, the founder of a new Gothic Rome. The Lombard kings ruled an Italy where consciousness of the Roman legacy was still strong; Rothari's specification of 17 kings looks suspiciously like an analogous attempt.

- The promulgation of written law codes by early medieval European kings had an ideological as well as a practical purpose: 'Germanic kings made laws, first and foremost, partly in order to emulate the literary legal culture of the Roman and Judaeo-Christian civilisation to which they were heirs, and partly to reinforce the links that bound a king or dynasty to their people'[98]. When the *Edict* is seen in this light, the close association of king-list and law code indicates that the two had a common purpose.

Putting these three considerations together, it seems highly probable that Rothari

---

[97] Wolfram 1967, 99-103 and 1968, 482-5
[98] Wormald 1977, 134-6

meant the king-list to be politically significant in some way. Given Rothari's situation[99], it is not difficult to see what that significance might have been. The Lombard kingdom in Italy was characterised by a constant tension among a large number of powerful dukedoms vying for the kingship. We have seen that certain families were able to enforce their hold over the kingship for successive generations, but a change of dynasty could, and demonstrably did, lead to unrest and even outright war. When, for example, the Gausi under Audoin took over the kingship from the long-established Lethingi, Hildigis, a member of the Lethingi, went into exile, recruited allies, and by a combination of intrigue and war almost succeeded in re-establishing himself and his family. For ten years between the end of the reign of Cleph (574) and the start of Authari's rule (584), there were no kings at all, and the Lombard kingdom looked as though it was going to devolve into numerous petty dukedoms. Rothari became king with the consent of his fellow *duces* after a period of turmoil. His family, the Harudi, had never held the kingship before. He needed to establish the coherence of the Lombard kingdom and his own authority over it, and the *Edict* was one way of doing this: he was of ancient aristocratic family, the latest in a long and illustrious line of Lombard kings, the giver of national law, and, for his Roman subjects, the initiator of great things to come.

Now, the clear implication of Rothari's stated intention to compile a written list of Lombard kings *propter futuris temporis memoria*, 'as a memorial for future times', is that it was being done for the first time, and consequently that the information which came to him *per antiquos homines*, 'from old men', did so via vernacular tradition. Two considerations support this. Firstly, the king-list gives the same succession of Lombard kings as that in the *Origo* and the *Historia*[100]. But we have seen that oral tradition about at least some of these kings was available in the seventh and eighth centuries. Rothari would, therefore, have

---

[99] Menghin 1985, 94-141
[100] Gschwantler 1976, 222 for textual relationships

had the relevant traditions to draw on if he so wished. Secondly, in issuing his *Edict*, Rothari was taking the radical step of reducing *antiquas legis patrum nostrorum quae scriptae non erant*, 'the ancient laws of our fathers which were not written down',[101] to writing for the first time. The terminology he uses to describe the literary redaction of previously unwritten law parallels that used to describe the compilation of the king-list. Where the list was produced *propter futuris temporis memoria*, the laws were to be observed *futuris temporibus firmiter et inviolibiliter*, 'firmly and without alteration in future times'; where the names of the kings *in hoc membranum adnotari iussimus*, 'we have commanded to be set down in this book', the law *in hoc membranum scribere iussimus*, 'we have commanded to write down in this book'; where Rothari got his information for the list *per antiquos homines*, the unwritten law on which the Edict is based represents what *per antiquos homines memorare potuerimus*, 'what we have been able to recall from old men'. In short, the process which produced the king-list closely parallels the process whereby orally-transmitted law was given literary form. The *antiqui homines* who provided the information about unwritten law also provided the material for the king-list. But we know what sort of material was available for the list. It therefore seems beyond reasonable doubt that Rothari used the same body of historical tradition as the compiler of the *Origo* and Paul the Deacon. This being so, the conclusion must be that Rothari used orally transmitted Lombard national historical tradition as a basis for royal propaganda.

One further step is possible. That Rothari used tribal tradition in this way must mean that, in the early seventh century, these traditions had an ideological significance for the Lombard aristocracy at whom the propaganda was directed. Were this not the case, it is difficult to see why Rothari would have bothered with such material at all, or how the propaganda which he based on it could have been effective. It is therefore interesting to note Paul the Deacon's comment that Theudelinda, the Bavarian wife of Agilulf (590-616) *built a palace in which she*

---

[101] Pertz 1868, 386

had painted something of the deeds of the Lombards[102]. On their own, Paul's words need be taken as no more than a comment on the queen's personal aesthetics, but in combination with what has been said about Rothari in the preceding discussion, it provides valuable corroboration that Lombard tribal traditions were known and esteemed in the royal court at the turn of the seventh century, just a few decades before Rothari produced his king-list. As such, his exploitation of this body of tradition can be seen in the context of a longer-term interest in it within the royal court.

---

[102] Waitz 1878, 4.22

d) THE FRANKS[103]

When we first hear of the Franks in the mid-third century AD they are settled to the north-east of the lower Rhine in present-day Holland and Germany, and are participating along with other Germanic groups in raids across the Roman frontier. At this stage, the Franks were seen by Roman observers as a confederation of peoples, though whether they saw themselves as an ethnic group is not known, and there is no indication that they formed any clearly defined political entity prior to the sixth century. By the early fourth century Franks had begun taking service in the Roman army, and several are known to have achieved high positions. In 350AD the Franks took part in an attack on the Roman frontier around Cologne and, after a successful Roman retaliation, a Frankish group, the Salians, were settled in Roman territory to the west of the Rhine where they stayed in relative obscurity until the later fifth century. Low-level warfare between other Frankish groups and the Romans continued to the end of the century. There is a particularly obscure period in the early fifth century, but in 451AD it is known that some Franks fought on the Roman side against Attila's Huns, and some on the Hunnish side. With the reign of Clovis (c.482 - 511 AD) came a turning point in Frankish fortunes. Building on the foundations laid by his predecessor and father Childeric, Clovis managed to bring most of Gaul under Frankish dominance and also to subject other groups in the Frankish confederation to his authority, so emerging as sole ruler of an extensive Frankish kingdom. With the further gains made by Clovis' four sons after his death, Frankish dominance over much of western Europe was secured for the dynasty that was in effect established by Childeric, the Merovingians. This Merovingian dominance lasted until 751 AD when Charles Martel, the grandfather of Charlemagne, ousted the last of the old line and installed the Carolingians in its place.

---

[103] This section is based on Zöllner 1970; Gerberding 1987, chs. 2 and 3; James 1988

i. Frankish lordship[104]

The groups which made up the Frankish 'confederation' prior to the rise of the Merovingians --Salii, Chamavi, Chattuarii, Chatti among others-- had leaders variously described in Roman sources as *duces, regales,* and *reguli;* there was no king (*rex*) of the Franks. Such leaders, like Tacitean *duces,* had retinues and led war bands or larger groupings, even peoples, to war. Writing in the late sixth century, Gregory of Tours derives the royal origin of the ruling dynasty of his own time, the Merovingians, from such *duces* in a famous passage: having crossed over to the left bank of the Rhine, he says, the Salian Franks *set up in each country district and city long-haired kings from the foremost and most noble family of their race.* This does not mean to say that this *most noble family* had been preeminent among other aristocratic Frankish families prior to or immediately following the Salian move westwards. It was Clovis who managed to establish a single kingship of the Franks by extensive conquest of non-Salian groups and by subsequent elimination of all the important collateral branches of his own family, thus restricting access to the kingship to his own line of descent. Under the Merovingian dynasty so established, the *dux* became an --in principle-- local lord subject to the Merovingian king, though with the growth in power of a now-settled aristocracy this subjection was by the seventh century often nominal. In the western part of the Frankish kingdom, where the Roman legacy was strong, the *dux* was lord over one or more *civitates;* in the more strongly barbarian east, the *duces* were associated with other ethnic groups, and were political and military leaders of confederations. By the later seventh and the eight centuries the more powerful *duces* had effectively become autonomous, but by the end of the eighth the reassertion of central control by Charlemagne suppressed this independence.

---

[104] Zöllner 1970, ch. 4; Wallace-Hadrill 1971, ch. 1; Wolfram 1971; James 1988; Barnwell

ii. Frankish historical tradition[105]

The first piece of evidence comes from Gregory of Tours' *Historia Francorum*. Gregory[106] was born into an aristocratic Gallo-Roman family in Clermont-Ferrand round about 540 AD. In 573 he became bishop of Tours, and in that position became influential in the ecclesiastical and political life of Gaul. The *Historia Francorum* was completed shortly before Gregory's death in 594 and, as its title indicates, deals with the history of the Franks from as far back as his sources allow up to his own time, and ends in 591. In treating of the earliest history of the Franks, Gregory musters all the information which Classical historiography has to offer, which is precious little; to it, he adds the following[107]:

> *Many say that, once they had left Pannonia and first came to inhabit the shores of the Rhine, they crossed the Rhine and traversed Thuringia, and there in each territory and city created long-haired kings from the foremost and most noble of their families.... They further tell that Chlogio was a useful and most noble king among that people, whose son was Childeric.*

From Gregory's explicit declaration that his written sources were exhausted, and from the words *tradunt, ferunt,* and *adserunt* which occur in the Latin text of the above passage, it is clear that this information came from historical tradition[108].

At the end of the account of Chlogio's career which follows the above passage, Gregory mentions that *some declare that Merowech was a king belonging to this line,* and then for no apparent reason launches into a tirade against heathenism: *But this race seems always to have been subject to mad religious practices...*[109]. The reason for this emerges on turning to the corresponding section in the *Chronicle of Fredegar*. On one view, the *Chronicle*

1997, ch.1
[105] On Frankish vernacular oral tradition see Richter 1994, chapters 5-7
[106] Brunhölzl 1975; Goffart 1988
[107] Krusch & Levison 1951, 57
[108] Hauck 1955, 197; Zöllner 1970, 110
[109] Krusch & Levison 1951, 58

of Fredegar[110] is a composite work of the seventh century: the first author completed the world chronicle section in 613 AD, the second added an excerpt from Books I - IV of Gregory's *Historia* in 642, and the third made additions and emendations to the work of the previous two in 658. Another view holds that the *Chronicle* is the work of a single compiler working with earlier materials, also during the seventh century. Its interest for present purposes is in the additions which the compiler(s) made to Gregory's information. Having followed Gregory in the passage just quoted, Fredegar adds an account of how Chlodio and his wife were on the seashore one day and, approached by *a creature of Neptune similar to the Minotaur* while she was swimming, that she became pregnant *either by the creature or by the man* and later gave birth to Merowech, from whom the Merovingians traced their origin[111]. In Greek mythology the Minotaur was half-man, half-bull, begotten on a human woman by the divine bull which Poseidon, the Greek equivalent of Neptune, had given to King Minos. The first step in assessing this passage must be to decide whether we are here dealing with a literary invention based on Classical mythology --which would of course make this material useless for present concerns-- or with an *interpretatio Romana* of a Frankish myth.

The indications are for the latter[112]. Firstly, literate Christian churchmen during the earliest period of Frankish rule in Gaul were concerned to lure a barbarous people away from pagan beliefs, not to give them new ones. Gregory was clearly aware of some association between Merowech and heathenism, and his reaction is symptomatic. Secondly, both Gregory and Fredegar imply a source in vernacular tradition: in the *Historia, some declare* that Merowech was in the same line of descent as Chlodio, and Fredegar begins his interpolated account with *ferunt,* 'it is related'. Our hypothetical literate mythologiser is therefore doubly

---

[110] Manitius 1911; Brunhölzl 1975; Fouracre & Gerberding 1996, 27
[111] Krusch 1888, 95
[112] On this material see Hauck 1955, 197-204; Hauck 1964, 30-32; Wallace-Hadrill 1971, 18; Höfler 1973

unlikely. Thirdly, and most importantly, the genealogical claims of the pagan Merovingian kings had religious observances connected with them. In 507 AD Avitus, bishop of Vienne 490-518, wrote a letter to Clovis on the occasion of the latter's baptism[113]. He began by praising the king for having embraced the Catholic faith. In doing so, Avitus goes on, Clovis has become a model for others who, brought to the brink of Christian conversion, set against it *the customary usage of their race and the ritual of their ancestral practice,* and thus *preserve a worthless reverence for their ancestors in the grip of unbelief,* giving as their excuse that they do not understand the issues involved in making the right choice. But this excuse, says Avitus, has with the baptism of Clovis ceased to be valid; Clovis, moreover, is now *satisfied with a nobility drawn solely from a lineage of ancient origin,* realising that he has through his baptism restored to his line of descent *whatever can adorn the whole summit of nobility.* In this part of the letter Avitus is concerned to reassure Clovis about the effects of Christian conversion on his *nobilitas.* Some aspect of it was lost: Clovis is now *satified with a nobilitas drawn* **solely** *from a lineage of ancient origin.* In other words, his pre-conversion *nobilitas* had consisted of something more than the antiquity of his line. What had been lost? By setting Clovis up as an example for those who wavered between paganism and Christianity, Avitus parallels their experience with his. They could, like him, lose a little but gain a great deal; he, like them, had originally resisted Christianity with *the customary usage of his race and the ritual of ancestral practice* and with *a worthless reverence for his ancestors in the grip of unbelief* . According to a contemporary witness, therefore, the pagan Merovingian king Clovis had claimed a *nobilitas* based only partly on antiquity of descent, and had had a reverence for his ancestors which involved ritual. Ritual presupposes a mythology, and moreover a mythology of native Frankish origin in this case; as we have seen, Gregory associates long-established cult practices with the name of Merowech.

---

[113] Peiper 1883, 75; on the letter see von den Steinen 1932-3, 480-94 and Hauck 1955, 199-204

If, then, Fredegar's story is taken as an *interpretatio Romana* of a pagan Frankish myth, there is good reason to think that both he and Gregory drew on a vernacular Frankish source. Gregory's narrative proceeds in quick succession from the above-quoted account of the early wanderings and kings of the Franks through the career of Chlodio to Merowech, and thence to a long diatribe against paganism. Into that narrative Fredegar inserts his Minotaur story which, on the above argument, is a pagan Frankish myth. But, to judge from Gregory's reaction, he was himself aware of some pagan association with the name of Merowech, and Fredegar's story is the natural candidate for that association. Now, we have seen the textual evidence that Gregory drew on vernacular tradition for his account of the earliest history of the Franks, and Fredegar's story on the present interpretation is necessarily taken from vernacular tradition. The indication, therefore, is that the entire sequence from early wanderings through Merowech, and including Fredegar's story, comes from vernacular Frankish tradition, and, given the subject matter, that that tradition was the Merovingian origin legend.

For explicit references to Frankish vernacular tradition we have to go to much later sources. The first and best known of these is Einhard's *Life of Charlemagne,* which says that Charlemagne *wrote down and committed to record barbarous and most ancient songs in which were sung the deeds and wars of past kings*[114]. Einhard[115] was born about 770 AD in the Main region of present-day Germany and, after being educated at Fulda, studied under Alcuin at Aachen. Thereafter he entered the service of Charlemagne and, later, of Charlemagne's successor Louis. About 830 he returned to a monastery in his native region, where he died about 840. He wrote his *Life of Charlemagne* between 829 and 836 AD on the model of Suetonius' *Lives of the Caesars,* that is, as a secular biography, and it is consequently an especially authoritative and informative source on its subject.

Associated with the Einhard passage is Theganus' comment that

---

[114] Waitz 1911, 33; commentary in Meissburger 1963
[115] Manitius 1911; Brunhölzl 1975

Charlemagne's son Louis *rejected the heathen poetical songs which he had learned in his youth, wishing neither to read, nor hear, nor teach them*[116]. Little is known of Theganus[117]. He was bishop of Trier, and completed a *Life* of Charlemagne's son Louis the Pious in 836 AD on, it is thought, the explicit pattern of Einhard's *Life*. And, finally, Poeta Saxo's *Life* of Charlemagne has the following to say about its subject[118]:

> *Begotten of famous men, he gleamed more brilliantly and shone forth more strongly than his invincible forebears; it is furthermore known that popular songs celebrate his fathers and ancestors with great praises, singing of Pippinus, Carolus, Hludowicus and Theodoricus, Carlomannus and Hlotharius.*

Poeta Saxo[119] is the name traditionally given to the anonymous author of a long epic poem, the *Gesta Caroli magni metrica,* written towards the end of the ninth century. Saxo depends for the most part on Einhard and on various annals, but occasionally he includes material not found in any other source. The kings celebrated in Saxo's *popular songs* are Carolingian and Merovingian. Carolus must be Charles Martel, Carlomannus a son of Charles', and Pippinus, another son of Charles', is Charlemagne's father[120]. The names Hludowicus and Hlotharius do not appear in the Carolingian family tree before Charlemagne's time, while the two Theodorics that do belong to a distant collateral branch. Saxo clearly had Clovis (Chlodowech) and his sons Theodoric and Chlothar in mind. That would make Merovingians ancestors of Carolingians, and so would appear to compromise the credibility of the above passage, but in fact there is no problem: ever since Pippin's

---

[116] Pertz 1829, 594
[117] Manitius 1911; Brunhölzl 1975
[118] de Winterfeld 1899, 58
[119] Manitius 1911; Brunhölzl 1975
[120] See the genealogical table in Braunfels 1966, 73-82

time the Carolingians had been concerned to link themselves genealogically with the Merovingians, whom they had supplanted[121].

At the turn of the eighth century and even as late as the early ninth, then, vernacular traditions articulated in song existed among the Franks. These songs were by then ancient, told of the deeds of kings of the past, and some at least of these kings were specifically Merovingian and Carolingian. The songs were, moreover, of sufficient interest to the Frankish royal family for the young prince Louis to have been taught them in his youth, and for his father to have taken the trouble to have them committed to writing.

Supplementing the evidence presented so far are passages in Gregory's *Historia* and in the *Liber Historiae Francorum* (completed 727 AD)[122] which, on stylistic grounds, were arguably taken from vernacular tradition. To present and discuss these passages here would be a lengthy undertaking. Rather than make the attempt, this discussion relegates them to a supporting role and refers the interested reader to work by Voretsch[123], who comprehensively collected and discussed a substantial corpus of material about Merovingian kings which, in his view, comes from vernacular sources. It is, however, worth commenting once again that while attribution of material in Latin texts to vernacular sources is a subjective affair, there is no logical reason why the writers of those texts should not have drawn on such sources, and there are cases, as in Paul the Deacon's *Historia Langobardorum,* where this is beyond reasonable doubt. One can question this or that in Voretsch's work, but is it hardly reasonable to dismiss the whole thing.

As with the Goths and Lombards, medieval *Heldensage* has some corroborative value. Hugdietrich and Wolfdietrich have traditionally been identified with Theodoric, the son of Clovis who died in 534 AD, and with Theodoric's son Theodebert (died 548), but these identifications are disputed. The

---

[121] Wenskus 1976
[122] Manitius 1911; Brunhölzl 1975; Fouracre & Gerberding 1996, 79 ff
[123] Voretsch 1896

Walter legend incorporates ostensibly Frankish characters, but whether they originally were Frankish is not now clear[124].

One further source of evidence needs to be considered. It comes from Venantius Fortunatus[125] (c.540 - c.600 AD), a native of northern Italy who crossed the Alps in 565 and travelled extensively in Frankish territory, finally becoming bishop of Poitiers. In his account of his wanderings in barbarian lands, he complains that his skills as a poet are little appreciated by people who cannot distinguish the squawking of a goose from the song of a swan, and where in the midst of drunken revelry *there is only the sound of the harp (arpa) thrumming out barbarous songs (barbaros leudos)*[126]. Despite that complaint, he composed numerous panegyrics for a variety of Frankish and Gallo-Roman aristocrats and clergymen. One such poem, composed around 567/8 AD while staying with King Sigibert at Metz and addressed to Lupus, a *dux* of Champagne[127], concludes as follows[128]:

> *The Roman praises you with the lyre, and the barbarian with*
> *the harp (harpa)... The latter calls you brave, the former*
> *powerful in justice; the latter praises your skill at arms, the*
> *former your learning. And, because a king has to have the*
> *accomplishments both of peace and war, the former celebrates*
> *his skill as a judge, and the latter as a battle leader. I give you*
> *verses, and the barbarian gives you songs called leudos: in*
> *these different ways the praise of one man resounds.*

The passage as a whole aims to contrast the sort of praise that Lupus gets from barbarian poetry with what he receives from civilised poets like Venantius himself, who is here concluding a poem lavish in its praise of Lupus. *Harpa* and

---

[124] Uecker 1972, 103-5 and 88-93

[125] Manitius 1911; Brunhölzl 1975; Brennan 1984, George 1992

[126] Leo 1888, Praefatio; see Richter 1994, 152-4

[127] On Lupus see George 1992), 79-82

[128] Leo 1888, VII.8, lines 63-72. On the Lupus poems see George 1992, 79 ff; on this passage in particular see Moisl 1981

leudos are Germanic words[129]: the first corresponds to OE *hearpe,* OHG *harpfa,* ON *harpa* and so on, and the second to OE *leoð,* OHG *liod,* ON *ljoð.* The barbarian court poet, therefore, is a Frank singing in the vernacular, and the songs he sings praise the warlike character of his patron. To judge from his general complaint about *barbaros leudos,* moreover, this kind of poetry was widespread in Frankish territory.

Venantius makes no connection between such panegyric verse and Frankish historical tradition. Its relevance to this discussion derives from the fact that, among other barbarian groups we shall be examining, court poets and panegyric are closely associated with historical tradition, and the above passage constitutes evidence that this might have been so among the Franks as well.

iii. Lordship and historical tradition among the Franks

Normally, in discussions of Einhard's famous comment on *the barbarous and most ancient songs* which Charlemagne collected, the passage is excerpted from the narrative without regard to its context and interpreted in terms which portray Charlemagne as a liberal antiquarian, concerned to preserve what is old as an end in itself, and perhaps even for the convenience of future literary scholars[130]. But the context is crucial. The passage comes just after Einhard has told how, having received the imperial title, Charlemagne reformed existing law codes and redacted the previously unwritten laws of the peoples under his dominion: it is clear that Einhard saw the writing down of the laws and of the *carmina* as related things. This invites comparison with what Rothari had done a century and a half earlier. Both kings were issuing definitive written law codes based, in whole or part, on law previously transmitted orally, and both were doing so to manifest their authority. Wormald[131] is surely right to see particular significance in the fact that Charlemagne only began his legal reforms after he had been made emperor.

---

[129] Holthausen 1963
[130] Meissburger 1963, 107-8 and 113; Wormald 1977, 128-9
[131] Wormald 1977, 128-9

Rothari prefaced his code with a king-list cum genealogy which he based on Langobardic vernacular tradition because he saw invocation of this material as a means of legitimizing his authority in the eyes of his subjects. We have just seen that Frankish vernacular tradition was current before, in, and after Charlemagne's time. Given the Langobardic precedent, Einhard's juxtaposition of Charlemagne's legal reforms with the literary redaction of *barbarous and most ancient songs in which were sung the deeds and wars of past kings* must be interpreted to mean that Charlemagne intended much the same thing as Rothari. In fact, the thrust of Charlemagne's propaganda must have been specifically genealogical. Frankish vernacular tradition included songs about Merovingian and Carolingian kings and, as noted, it was Carolingian policy to associate themselves genealogically with the Merovingian dynasty. A literary redaction of Frankish vernacular tradition would, under the circumstances, have amounted to writing family history[132].

---

[132] Further on this in Meissburger 1963, 114 ff.

e) THE ANGLO-SAXONS[133]

The Germanic groups which settled Britain came from coastal regions of present-day Belgium, Holland, northern Germany, and Scandinavia. There were German mercenaries in Britain even during the Roman period, settled near major towns and roads and serving in the army. The Romano-British lords of the post-Roman period continued the policy of hiring Germans as mercenaries, but it appears to have backfired and been one of the factors which precipitated large-scale Germanic settlements in Britain, which began in earnest during the fifth century and continued into the sixth. By the time reasonably informative written records start to appear in the seventh century, the full extent of Germanic settlement was nearly complete, and only territories bordering on present-day Cornwall, Wales, Cumbria, and Scotland remained to be settled: Cumbria became Germanic, the rest remained Celtic, and so it has largely remained. A good deal is known about the progress of the Anglo-Saxon settlement, and it is an active area of research[134] but the details do not matter for present purposes.

i. Anglo-Saxon lordship[135]

When the non-literate continental Germanic peoples were living in their forests beyond the *limes,* or raiding in Imperial territory, or fighting amongst themselves, or migrating, or settling, there were literate Romans to describe them. The relatively uninformative Gildas excepted, no such descriptions exist for the period of Anglo-Saxon migration into Britain, and as a result there is no direct evidence for the development of Anglo-Saxon lordship in the fifth and sixth centuries. When documentation becomes available in the seventh, the most visible facts of the Anglo-Saxon political scene are a group of relatively large kingdoms-- Deira, Bernicia, Mercia and the like-- and, for each such kingdom, a single royal

---

[133] Sawyer 1978, ch. 1

[134] Bassett 1989b; Yorke 1990

[135] This section depends on Bassett 1989b; Charles-Edwards 1989; Yorke 1990; Higham 1995; Barnwell 1997, ch. 4

dynasty with exclusive rights to the kingship. Above this political level, it was occasionally possible for an especially successful king to assert overlordship over one or more of his peers. Below it were lords variously described in the sources as *reguli, subreguli, principes,* and *duces,* some of them members of the king's own family, some rulers of subject kingdoms, and some *duces* in the Tacitean sense of battle leaders who, depending on how successful they were, could aspire to establish a stable domain. All of them owed allegiance to the king, but could themselves exercise control over subsidiary lords, and so on recursively. What emerges is an --untidy-- tree structure of overlordships with small, probably tribal lords at the leaves and the occasional overlord *bretwalda* at the root.

ii. **Anglo-Saxon historical tradition**

Compared to what is available for the Germanic peoples discussed so far, the evidence for historical tradition and its relation to lordship among the Anglo-Saxons is quite abundant and varied. At its core is a group of three Old English poems --*Beowulf, Widsið,* and *Deor*-- which jointly offer a comprehensive account of the relation between lordship and tradition, and of the court poet's role as custodian of that tradition. The discussion to follow deals first of all with these poems, presenting the information which they offer and assessing their historical reliability. It then goes on to consider the remaining material, again assessing reliability. Finally, the two categories of evidence are compared with a view to determining the extent to which they agree.

Old English poetry: *Beowulf, Widsið,* and *Deor*

This section presents the information offered by the above three poems. The immediately subsequent section then addresses the issue of their historical reliability. At present, all that needs to be said about them is that all three are preserved in unique manuscript copies of c.1000 AD.

Beowulf[136]

For present purposes, *Beowulf* can be regarded as a literary evocation of aristocratic life in migration-age southern Scandinavia. Its setting can be quite precisely determined. Geographically, the action of the poem is divided between Denmark and Götland. Chronologically we are in the early sixth century: the poem contains a reference to a Danish raid on the northern coast of the Frankish kingdom which is also mentioned by Gregory of Tours, and which Gregory dates to c.520 AD[137]. The poem describes a world in which numerous more or less independent peoples coexist in a chronic state of low-level warfare with one another. These peoples are ruled by royal dynasties whose primary function is to defend their kingdoms against external aggression and, wherever possible, to subjugate their neighbours. Kings are essentially warlords who lead personal retinues of professional warriors, and to whom they are bound by reciprocal obligations: the king maintains his men in peacetime by entertaining them in his court and providing for their support by gifts, and the men reciprocate by bravery and utter loyalty in war. Success in war means increased status and wealth, which attracts a larger retinue, which in its turn makes victory more likely: war is the engine of Beowulfian kingship. Succession to this kingship is open to members of the royal dynasty of the group in question, and is achieved by the dynast who is able both to demonstrate martial prowess and generosity --the primary qualifications for kingship-- and to muster a retinue, allies, and wealth sufficient to enforce his claim. To demonstrate all this, we shall look first at the Danish and then at the Geatish kings in the poem.

Beowulf begins with a sequence of Danish kings who are bound in explicit genealogical relationship and constitute the first four generations of a dynasty, the Scyldingas[138]: Scyld, its eponymous ancestor, is succeeded by his son Beow, who is in turn followed by his own son Healfdene; Healfdene has four children one of

---

[136] All references are to Klaeber 1950
[137] Krusch and Levison 1951, III.3
[138] On the Scyldingas see Newton 1993

whom, Hroþgar, becomes king after him; later in the poem the tenure of the Scyldingas is extended to a fifth generation by the accession of Hroþulf, Hroþgar's nephew (lines 1-85). Scyld exemplifies the king's primarily martial role. He *dragged the mead benches away from bands of foes* and *flourished beneath the skies, prospered in honours, so that every one of those who dwelt around him across the whale's road had to obey him, pay him tribute. That was a good king* (lines 4-11). In Beow we see how a king's primary function as defender of the people depended on his securing the loyalty of a retinue by generosity in gift-giving: (lines 20-25)

> *So it is that a young man, while still in his father's protection,*
> *ought to do good deeds, making liberal rich gifts, so that when*
> *he comes of age good companions will stand by him, lend aid*
> *to the people when war comes.*

Of Beow's successor Healfdene we learn only that he, too, had been a warrior: *He ruled the noble Scyldings for as long as he lived, old and savage in war* (lines 57-8); his successor Hroþgar is introduced by a passage that is in effect a definition of the dynamics of Beowulfian kingship (lines 64-81):

> *Then success in war, glory in battle, was granted to Hroþgar,*
> *so that his kinsmen gladly obeyed him until the youthful band*
> *of companions grew into a mighty troop of young warriors. It*
> *came into his mind that he would instruct men to build a mead*
> *hall greater than any that men had ever heard of, and therein*
> *to distribute to young and old everything which God had given*
> *him...I have heard how orders for the work were given to many*
> *people throughout the world to adorn the nation's palace. So,*
> *in time, rapidly as men reckon, it was completed, the greatest*
> *of halls. He who ruled widely with his words gave it the name*
> *Heorot. He did not neglect his vow; he distributed rings and*
> *treasures at the banquet.*

Hroþgar acquires a reputation for martial prowess as a young man, and so attracts a large retinue. This enables him, like his ancestor Scyld, to subjugate neighbouring peoples --*he ruled widely with his words*-- and is able to command *many peoples throughout the world* to finance and build his hall, the symbol of his ascendancy, in which he rewards the men who helped him attain that position and thereby, like Beow, secures their continuing loyalty. In the narrative that follows Hroþgar is repeatedly described as the guardian of his kingdom: he is the *helm Scyldinga, rices weard, eþelweard, rices hyrde, leodgebyrga;* summing up his reign, he says: *For a hundred seasons I ruled the Ring-Danes beneath the skies, secured them from war by spear and sword-edge against many nations throughout the world, so that I did not reckon on any opponent under the expanse of heaven (*lines 1769-73). By the time we meet him Hroþgar and his court are no longer what they were, and are in fact powerless against the monster Grendel, but he is still given such titles as *guðcyning, sigedryhten,* and *hilderinc,* and there are harkings back to his former prowess: *When Healfdene's son wished to take part in the play of swords, the valour of the far-famed man never failed him at the front when the slaughtered were falling* (lines 1040- 42). But *old age ...took him from the joys of strength* (lines 1886-7), and whereas in his youth he *held a broad kingdom, a rich stronghold of heroes* (lines 466-7), his hall troop had shrunk. Hroþgar remains generous, however. He is the *beahhorda weard, sinces brytta, goldwine gumena* --the best of earthly kings among the seas, of those who distributed wealth in the Danish realm (lines 1684-6)-- and his hall is the *gifhealle, goldsele,* and his throne the *gifstol.* Unable to overcome Grendel and his mother alone, Hroþgar promises Beowulf rich rewards for his help, and, observing that he has *often enough conferred rewards for lesser deeds, honouring with riches a slighter warrior, weaker in combat* (lines 951-3), Hroþgar delivers lavishly: gold, weapons, armour, horses, trappings.

Though there is no explicit genealogy of Geatish kings corresponding to the Scylding one, it is easily seen that among the Geatas, too, kingship was the prerogative of a single royal dynasty. The earliest king mentioned in the poem is Hreþel, who had three sons Herebald, Hæþcynn, and Hygelac. The first died while still a prince, the second succeeded his father, and after his death was in his turn followed by his brother Hygelac. After Hygelac was killed in battle, his son Hearded became king, after which tenure switches to the female line of descent from Hreþel in the person of Beowulf, Hygelac's nephew via a daughter of Hreþel's (17); as he lay dying, Beowulf designated his closest kinsman Wiglaf his heir (lines 2809-16).

Of Hreþel we know only that he raised his grandson Beowulf at his court and, says Beowulf, *gave me treasure at the banquet* (lines 2430-31); his son and successor was a warrior, for he died in battle (lines 2435-40). Hygelac is less obscure. Like Hroþgar he is the guardian of his people --*folces hyrde, eorla hleo*-- and fulfills this function primarily as a battle leader: a *guðcyning* and *heaþorof cyning*, he dies leading an attack on the Franks (from line 2914). Hygelac presides over his retinue in a court whose members he maintains with treasure and land. Again like Hroþgar, he is a *sinces brytta*, and his hall is the place where *the great young war king was dealing out rings in the stronghold* (lines 1966- 70). For their services against the Swedes, for example, he repaid two of his men *for that battle onslaught with copious treasures, he bestowed on each of them a hundred thousand's worth of land and linked rings...after they had achieved fame by fighting* (lines 2991-98). Beowulf is himself *Hygelaces þegn* (line 194), and receives both treasure and land from him. In return he fights loyally for his lord: *I repaid with my bright sword in battle the treasure which he bestowed on me. He gave me estate, a dwelling..I would always go before him in the troop* (lines 2490-93). When Beowulf eventually succeeds to the kingship he is, like his predecessor, a *folces weard.* Looking back on a long reign he declares: *There was no nation's king among those dwelling round who dared approach me with allies in war, threaten with terror'* (lines 2733-36). That role is crucial to the survival of the people. On Hygelac's death the queen offers Beowulf the kingship because her son is still too young *to hold the throne of the homeland against foreign nations* (lines 2369-72). Little need be said about Beowulf's martial prowess. It suffuses the poem. As a prince he had had a small and loyal retinue (line 207): when Grendel burst into Heorot *many a warrior drew out an ancient heirloom, wished to defend the life of the noble leader* (lines 794-97). When he became king, Beowulf maintained these men at his court. Like Hygelac and Hroþgar, he is described as a *goldgyfa*, a *goldwine*, and he sits on the *gifstol Geata;* as he lies dying, he rejoices that he has been able to win the dragon's treasure for his people, even if it was at the cost of his life (lines 2794-2801). His generosity is, however, ill repaid when his men desert him at the final dragon fight. His one loyal retainer and prospective heir, Wiglaf, castigates them for failing in their obligations to their lord, and predicts ruin for them: *Now the receiving of treasure and giving of swords, all delight of native land, beloved home, must cease for your race* (lines 2884-86).

Associated with Beowulfian kingship is a type of court poet that generates and propagates historical tradition[139]. He is mentioned four times in the poem. The first reference is part of the evocation of the Scylding royal hall in all its splendour just prior to the coming of Grendel, and presents the poet, the *scop,* as an integral part of court life (lines 86-90):

> *Then the powerful demon who abode in the darkness found it*
> *hard to endure the torment, when every day he heard loud*
> *rejoicing in the hall. There was the sound of the harp, the*
> *clear song of the scop.*

Again, on Beowulf's arrival at Hrothgar's court, benches are cleared for him and his men, ale is poured, and the feasting begins: *From time to time the scop sang clear-voiced in Heorot* (lines 496-97). What the *scop* sang emerges

---

[139] On the poet in *Beowulf* see Opland 1976

from the third of the four references. The occasion is yet another feast in Heorot, this time to celebrate the killing of Grendel (lines 1063-67):

There, in the presence of Healfdene's battle leader, song and music
were joined together, the joyful wood was plucked, a story
often rehearsed, when, to entertain the hall, the scop would
recite along the mead benches.

A paraphrase of one of these stories then follows. It is the Finnsburg Episode, a complicated tale of fighting and oath breaking between Finn, king of the Frisians, and a group of Danes who were visiting the court; it ends: *The song, the scop's lay, was sung.* Now, the Danish expedition to Finnsburg was led by one Hnæf, who was a Scylding (line 1069) and thus a member of the dynasty to which Hroþgar himself belonged. What we have here is an example of a court poet reciting an episode from his patron's dynastic history in the royal hall. That episode stresses the martial prowess of Hnæf, and the mutual loyalty of Hnæf and his men; that the Scyldingas had a dynastic history is confirmed by the narrative genealogy with which *Beowulf* opens.

The fourth and final time the poet appears is in the morning after Beowulf has driven Grendel out of Heorot. Hroþgar and his men follow Grendel's tracks (lines 853-86)[140]:

From there old companions, and many a young man also,
returned from the joyful journey, riding from the lake,
high-spirited on horseback, warriors on glossy steeds. Then
Beowulf's fame was proclaimed. Many repeatedly declared that
nowhere in the wide world, north or south between the seas, was
there any shield-bearer nobler than he under the expanse of
heaven, nor more worthy of power...At times one of the king's
thanes, a man full of high-sounding words, with a memory for

---

[140] On the interpretation of this passage, with references to earlier commentary on it, see Opland 1980b

stories, who remembered a multitude of old legends, improvised
a new poem linked in true metre. The man began by his art to
relate Beowulf's exploit and skilfully to tell an apt tale, varying
his words. He spoke of all he had heard tell about Sigemund,
about courageous deeds, many strange things - of the struggle
of the son of Wæls, his remote journeys, feuds and crimes, about
which the children of men knew little except for Fitela, of whom
he would speak of such matters, as uncle to nephew, since they
were always friends in need in every conflict; they laid low with
their swords many of the race of ogres. No little glory (dom)
accrued to Sigemund after the day of his death, since, bold in
battle, he had slain a dragon...

A description of Sigemund's dragon adventure then follows. This *king's thane* is the *scop* of the other three passages. The account of how he composed the *spel*, the story of Beowulf's exploit *--word oðer fand, soðe gebunden, ongan...wordum wrixlan--* has long been seen as a description of mnemonic composition and oral recitation in the pan-Germanic alliterative style; the thane's designation of *gleoman* is elsewhere a synonym for *scop* (the identification is discussed further in what follows). On the one hand, then, this poet has an extensive repertoire of historical narrative: he is a *guma gilphlæden, gidda gemyndig, se ðe ealfela ealdgesegena worn gemunde,* the nature of which is exemplified in the adventures of Sigemund, a legendary hero of the Germanic past. On the other, he composes extempore a new poem which publicly celebrates the exploits of a contemporary hero

In composing the poem in praise of his exploit against Grendel, the poet was realising Beowulf's primary motivation: a commitment to the acquisition of lasting personal fame. This commitment is most strikingly articulated in Beowulf's dying wish (lines 2802-08):

Bid those famous in war to build a fine mound over the pyre
on the headland by the sea It shall tower high on the Whale's

Cape as a remembrance to my people, so that seafarers, when they drive their tall ships from afar across the mists of the flood, will thereafter call it Beowulf's Barrow.

The ideology of personal fame through mighty exploits is represented in *Beowulf* by the striving for *dom*. *Dom* is a nominal formation from the same root as Old English *deman*, 'to judge', and though it is usually glossed as 'fame' or 'glory' it is more accurately rendered as 'judgment' and, in the context of the poem, as the judgment accorded an individual by his fellows, the estimation in which he stands. The central importance of *dom* for Beowulf emerges from the words which he utters just as he is about to embark on an adventure which looks likely to cost him his life: *For each of us there is an end to life in this world. Let him who can achieve dom before his death. That is best for a man after he is gone* (lines 1386-89). *Dom* is acquired primarily by martial prowess. This is implicit in the passage just quoted, and explicit in several others. Beowulf, the exemplary hero, wins *dom* not against human foes but by killing monsters invincible to anyone but himself. Thus, after he has driven Grendel out of Heorot, Hroþgar tells him: *You have ensured with deeds that your dom will live forever* (lines 953-55). Prior to going after Grendel's mother, Beowulf declares: *I shall achieve dom for myself...or death will take me* (lines 1490-91); he returns *a man brave in deeds, ennobled by dom* (line 1645), and Hroþgar is justly able to say on Beowulf's departure: *Your fame, my friend Beowulf, is exalted in every nation throughout distant regions* (lines 1703-05). Later in the poem, as an old man, Beowulf still has the same spirit. Having decided to attack the dragon, he says: *I engaged in many a war in my youth. An old guardian of the people, I will seek out the feud, a famous deed. . .or else war will take your lord* (lines 2511 - 15, 2535-37); during the actual battle, his loyal retainer Wiglaf urges him to fight on by saying: *In the days of your youth, you said that you would never let your dom perish while you were alive* (lines 2664-66*)*. The poem in praise of Beowulf, then, realised his commitment to lasting fame by providing a medium whereby his *dom* was proclaimed among contemporaries.

But panegyric in Beowulf's world does more than this. An initially curious feature of the passage under discussion is that, in a poem celebrating Beowulf's victory over Grendel, the *scop* should start telling about Sigemund, a legendary hero of the distant past, and in particular that Sigemund had slain a dragon, thereby achieving *great dom after his death.* Why should he do this? In killing Grendel, Beowulf achieved something very like Sigemund's deed, and, as we saw, acquired great *dom* for it. It is clear that the *scop* intended a parallel between the two heroes, saying in effect that Beowulf was the equal of the great hero of the past, and that his *dom,* like Sigemund's would last. But Sigemund's *dom* lived precisely in the historical narrative poetry of which the *scop* was the custodian; the implication is that Beowulf's would live on in this way too. And how would this come about? By the poem which the *scop* was composing at that very moment. Panegyric verse thus emerges as a medium for the propagation and generation of historical tradition. On the one hand, the poem in praise of Beowulf assesses him in traditional terms --he is compared to a great hero of the past. On the other, poetry praising his *dom* could enter the corpus of historical narrative which was transmitted by successive generations of *scopas.*

Widsið

Widsið is of particular interest for this study because it is specifically about court poets[141]. There are two speakers in the poem: a poet named Widsið, whose account of his experiences makes up the bulk of it, and a narrator who introduces Widsið at the beginning and makes some general observations about court poets at the end. Discussion of the poem will be in three parts: the narrator's introduction, Widsið's account, and the narrator's epilogue.

---

[141] Malone 1962; for commentary see Howlett 1974, 9

The narrator introduces Widsið as one who *had travelled around most of the nations of men, of peoples, in the world,* and, for reasons that are not explained at this stage, *often received splendid treasures in the hall.* He goes on to say, rather indirectly, that Widsið belonged to a people called the Myrgingas, that he set out on his travels *from the east, from Angeln,* and that his destination was *the home of Hreðcyning, of Eormenric, foe of treaty breakers.* The Myrgingas are very probably to be located in the region of present-day southern Denmark or northernmost Germany[142]; it emerges later in the poem that the Eormenric in question is the fourth-century king of the Visigoths. Widsið, therefore, moves in a migration-age Germanic world.

Widsið begins his speech with some very general observations about lordship, which he follows with a long list of rulers who were good lords. Thereafter he describes his journey to Eormenric's court, his travels within the Gothic kingdom, and his eventual return home. He claims in the course of that journey to have visited a great many other peoples of the *Völkerwanderung* period, and to have stayed with the rulers of several of these: Guðhere king of the Burgundians (early sixth century), Ælfwine king of the Lombards (later sixth century), Eormenric king of the Goths (mid-later fourth century) and a variety of other Gothic leaders of the fourth, fifth, and sixth centuries. As such, Widsið's account reiterates the narrator's prologue in making him a figure of the migration period; the significance of the fact that the rulers he allegedly visited were not contemporary will emerge in due course.

Widsið depicts himself as a poet who performs in the various courts he visits, and who receives gifts of treasure in exchange. We have already seen him described as having *often received splendid treasures in the hall.* He himself makes the same claim several times. Having come to the Burgundian Guðhere's court, he says: *There I received a ring. There Guðhere gave me goodly treasure in reward for my song. He was not an ungenerous king.* Eormenric, he says,

---

[142] Malone 1962, 183-6

rewarded me well, giving *an ornament that was reckoned at 600 sceattas of refined gold.* He was also *in Italy with Ælfwine. Of all men he had, as I have heard, the most generous hand for winning of praise, the most liberal heart for giving of rings.*

The songs for which Widsið was rewarded celebrated the generosity of his royal patrons. This is hinted at in the passage about Ælfwine just quoted; in the Gothic court he not only received treasure from Eormenric, but from the queen as well:

> *Her praise reached throughout many lands when I told in song*
> *where under the heavens I knew the best gold-adorned queen to be*
> *giving treasure. Then Scilling and I with a bright voice raised up a*
> *song before our victorious lord, loud with the harp our singing*
> *resounded. Then many men, proud in spirit, those who well knew*
> *spoke with words, and said that they had never heard a better song*

Widsið's song not only praised the queen's generosity before the immediate court, but made her famous *throughout many lands.* This latter effect appears to have been achieved by Widsið reciting her praise in other courts he visited: *I travelled around many foreign lands,* he says. *I can sing and relate stories, tell before the multitude in the mead hall how the well born ones rewarded me with gifts.*

Widsið's account also offers some information about the poet's status in the court. So far, everything points to his being an itinerant minstrel who travels from court to court and is paid for his services. But consider what happened when he finally returned to his own people with the treasure he had collected:

> *I was with Eormenric throughout his reign. There the king of the*
> *Goths rewarded me well. The king of the fortress dwellers gave me*
> *an ornament reckoned at 600 sceattas of refined gold. That I gave*
> *into the keeping of Eadgils, my protecting lord, the lord of the*

Myrgingas, when I returned home, to the dear one in exchange for
the land he gave me, for the estate of my father.

Beowulf elucidates the significance of this. There, as we saw, kings maintained their retinues in peacetime. Part of that maintenance was land. This land was the retainer's at the king's pleasure: it was granted for service, and could be withdrawn if the service was unsatisfactory, as the retainers who had deserted Beowulf found (lines 2884-2890). Beowulf, a member of Hygelac's retinue, went abroad to prove himself as a warrior, and returned home with the treasure that was the visible token of his achievement. He offered this treasure to Hygelac, whose response was to grant him a large estate (lines 2190-2199). Widsið's case is parallel. He enters service abroad, and returns home with treasure that betokens his achievement not as a warrior but as a poet. This he offers to his lord Eadgils, who regrants him his father's estate in exchange. Taking *Beowulf* as a guide, it looks as though Widsið, the son of a royal retainer who held land from his lord, followed in his father's footsteps and served in the retinue as his lord's court poet.

We turn now to the epilogue of the poem, which reads as follows:

So, travelling about, the poets of men move according to their
destinies among many lands. They speak their need, say words of
thanks, and always, north or south, they encounter one who
appreciates poetry, generous in giving, who wishes to display his
dom before the troop, to manifest his lordship, until all things pass
away, light and life both. He wins praise for himself, and has
eternal dom under the heavens.

Widsið has been speaking in the past tense. The narrator now speaks in the present. In these final lines, he is drawing a parallel between Widsið and the poets of his own day. Like Widsið, these poets travel from court to court seeking patronage. Also like him, they offer poetry; given the explicit parallel, the implication is that this poetry, like Widsið's, celebrates generosity. Such verse offers the patron the means to *display dom before the troop*, and thus to achieve two effects: on the one hand, he thereby *manifests his lordship,* and on the other he *wins praise for himself, and has eternal dom under the heavens.*

To understand why verse in praise of generosity should *manifest lordship* we have to look back at what has been said about kingship and *dom* in *Beowulf.* There, *dom* is acquired primarily by fighting; because martial prowess is one of the two main attributes of kingship in the poem, to display *dom* is to display royal credentials. But the other main attribute of kingship in *Beowulf* is generosity and, not surprisingly, it brings *dom* as well: the Danish king Heremod was niggardly, and *did not give rings to the Danes in accordance with dom* (lines 1719-20). In celebrating generosity the court poet of *Widsið* was manifesting lordship as surely as the *scop* in *Beowulf* was in celebrating bravery.

The key to understanding why the narrator thought that celebrating generosity could immortalise *dom* lies in the realisation that, when *Widsið* in its present form was composed, the kings and peoples whom the poet Widsið visits were the stuff of legend. The Anglo-Saxon who composed *Widsið* created two characters. He set one of them, Widsið, in the world of that legend, and the other, the narrator, in the present. Through the narrator, he says that poets like Widsið were continuing to function, and in particular that they continued to offer their patrons eternal *dom.* Widsið had made good that promise: he had celebrated rulers of the distant past, and they now lived on in legend. By implication, the *dom* of a contemporary lord who patronises a court poet will live on in such legend himself. So, as in *Beowulf,* panegyric is a mechanism for the generation of historical tradition.

Deor

Deor is a relatively short poem in which a *scop* laments the loss of his long-held position as court poet. The structure, unusually, is stanzaic. In each of the first four stanzas the poet alludes to some great sorrow in heroic legend, and ends with a refrain that is notoriously difficult to translate precisely, but means something like: *That passed, so may this.* The fifth stanza is a general meditation on fate. In the sixth, the poet tells us about himself[143]:

> *I will say this about myself, that I was for a time the scop of the Heodeningas, dear to my lord; my name was Deor. For many winters I had a good position in the retinue, a good lord, until Heorrenda, a man skilled in song, now enjoys the rights to the land which the protector of men had previously given me. That passed away, so may this.*

The Heodeningas, like *Widsið's* Myrgingas, were a small migration-age people of northern Germany, and Heorrenda appears in medieval *Heldensage* as a great poet of the Germanic past --a sort of Germanic Homer[144]. The *scop* who speaks in *Deor*, therefore, sets himself in the same migration-age world as those in *Beowulf* and *Widsið.*

Before his dismissal Deor had been a long-term member of his lord's retinue, and had enjoyed land-rights commensurate with that position: he had had *a folgað*, 'membership of the retinue', and a lord who had given him *londryht*, 'rights to land'. Like the retainers who deserted Beowulf in his fight with the dragon, however, he lost his position together with the land that went with it when his lord was no longer satisfied with his service.

As regards the sort of poetry he cultivated, not much can be inferred from Deor's description of Heorrenda as a *leoðcræftig mon*, 'a man skilled in the craft of song'. In citing great tragedies from heroic legend, though, he displays a repertoire of traditional material.

Discussion

The accounts which these three poems give of court poets and their poetry are not only mutually consistent but also overlap in many respects. They set the

---

[143] Malone 1977, 27
[144] Malone 1977, 39

court poet in a relatively small geographical area of northern Germany and southern Scandinavia in the late Germanic migration age. In all of them, the poet's natural place is in the lord's hall on festive occasions; *Widsið* and *Deor* make him a full land-holding member of the patron's retinue, whom he served not by fighting like the other retainers, but with his verse. That verse falls into two categories: (i) panegyric and (ii) historical tradition, including royal dynastic history. Panegyric realised the aristocratic desire for fame by praising the individual for his personal qualities and, at least sometimes, by comparsion with great men of the past. It also served to generate new historical tradition which could then be propagated by successive generations of poets.

Two questions arise, however. Firstly, all the poems survive in unique manuscript copies dating from c.1000AD, but they describe a world half a millennium in the past. How reliable is what they say about court poets and their poetry for that time? And secondly, the poets and poetry they describe are set in northern continental Germany and southern Scandinavia: even if their information could be shown to be accurate, how is it relevant to Anglo-Saxon England? On the face of it, the poems inspire little confidence either as reliable historical records or --despite their being Old English poems-- as sources of information for Anglo-Saxon England. We shall look briefly at why this is so, and then go on to argue that their evidence is nevertheless authoritative for present concerns.

Certain broad generalisations can be made about Old English poetry[145]. The one that looms largest in my mind is the vastness of the scholarly literature attached to the 33,000 or so lines of verse which survive. From the birth of Germanic philology in the nineteenth century to the literary-critical industry generated by university English departments all over the world since the 1950s, the number of learned investigations into every aspect of the corpus has grown steadily and, in the 1960s and 1970s, even alarmingly. Moreover, whereas scholarly and research literature in other disciplines is eventually superseded, the

---

[145] On Old English poetry in general see Alexander 1983

rate of attrition in Old English studies is very low, and it is common to refer to work many decades old. The consequence is that no individual can now credibly claim to know all or even most of what there is to know about Old English poetry, despite the relatively small size of the primary corpus.

The preceding paragraph articulates a complaint born of frustration, but that is not its main purpose. Literary-historical scholarship is about inference from evidence, and the consequent statement of generalisations over that evidence. As the volume of scholarly literature grows beyond what one individual can reasonably expect to read and digest, such generalisations become increasingly difficult to make with conviction. The cost, in terms of bibliographical search and reading, can easily become excessive, and it can be easier to leave the generalisation unmade. In such a situation, unfounded notions can easily establish themselves and become part of the presuppositional framework of the discipline. The notion I have in mind is that Old English poetry can, in general, be dated and in some cases even localised with acceptable reliability[146]. However, with a very few exceptions, such as *Caedmon's Hymn,* the *Battle of Maldon,* and the *Chronicle* poems, this is simply not the case at present. In what follows, this sweeping assertion is substantiated with reference to the poem which, more than any other, exemplifies the situation: *Beowulf.*

Bede provides a context for *Caedmon's Hymn*[147], and with it dating and localisation criteria; the *Battle of Maldon*[148] refers to an independently known historical event in a specific part of England. Where such evidence is lacking, as it is in most cases, linguistic features of the extant text which are held to have chronological and/or geographical implications are the primary criterion, together with, sometimes, general historical arguments for the plausibility of some particular time and place. One way to substantiate the assertion made in the preceding paragraph would be guerrilla warfare through these linguistic and

---

[146] Dumville 1981
[147] Colgrave and Mynors 1969, III/5
[148] Gordon 1976

plausibility arguments. There is, however, a simple observation which obviates the need for that: an Old English poem is what exists in a manuscript, not what has gone into its making. To see the implications of this, consider *Beowulf.* It survives in a manuscript dated c.1000 AD, and contains material which derives ultimately from sixth-century Scandinavia. What happened to the material between its genesis and the redaction of the manuscript copy of the poem? One cannot reasonably doubt there there was a more or less lengthy period of oral tradition for at least some of the content. How long was that period, and what happened to the traditions during that time? How did the traditions get to England? When were they first written down? Did oral and literary forms of the traditions exist side by side and, if so, how if at all did they interact? Were the traditions always structured as they presently are in the manuscript poem? If not, when was this structure first imposed on them? What were the poet's motivations? What effect did these motivations have on the material? Does the manuscript copy preserve the original *Beowulf*-poem accurately and, if not, what changes were made? Is there any reason to think that there was an earlier *Beowulf* on which the manuscript copy is based? And so on. Answers to such questions have been attempted often enough, but, as the best of these attempts admit[149], the results have been generally inconclusive. The problem is that we simply do not have enough information to be able to answer them with any reasonable degree of certainty. That being so, the only safe --indeed respectable-- course is to treat *Beowulf* as a late tenth or early eleventh century copy of an unlocalised Anglo-Saxon work dating from between c.700 and c.1000AD. *Beowulf* might be seventh century[150], or eighth century[151], or perhaps later, but we have no way of

---

[149] For example Wormald 1978; Chase 1981; Dumville 1981; Newton 1993; Kiernan 1996
[150] Girvan 1971
[151] Whitelock 1957

knowing which, or what it looked like at those times[152]; what we do know is what it looked like c.1000. Analogous arguments apply to most Old English poems, including *Deor* and *Widsið*.

Our three poems, moreover, belong to the *Heldensage* genre[153], and there has been a good deal of scholarly work over the years on the genesis and historical reliability of that genre, little of which is encouraging. Examples of *Heldensage* are attested in several western European medieval vernacular literatures, and date from, in principle, between the onset of literacy in the wake of Christian conversion to the fifteenth century. All the texts belonging to this genre have this in common: they deal with characters and events of the so-called Germanic *Völkerwanderung* period between about 300 and 600 AD, and are based ultimately on oral tradition originating during that period. To a greater or lesser degree they all offer information not only about persons and events of migration-age Germanic peoples, but also about such things as political and social institutions as well as material culture, often in seductive detail. Despite its basis in history, however, *Heldensage* is at best a delphic historical source[154]. Distortions of history occurred at the outset. On the one hand, the central argument of this discussion is that the historical traditions which European barbarian peoples cultivated were more of a propaganda medium subject to politically motivated manipulation than a dispassionate historical record. On the other, contemporary events were rendered in terms of canonical narrative structures[155]. As these traditions were propagated in the course of the early medieval centuries, opportunities for further distortion multiplied. By the time the first vernacular *Heldensage* texts appear, the traditions had moved beyond the territorial boundaries of the peoples which had originated them --or, where the peoples disappeared, as in the case of the Goths, survived their demise-- and became cultural material common the the Germanic-speaking

---

[152] See comments by Stanley in Chase 1981, 197 ff

[153] Schneider 1962; von See 1972; Uecker 1972; Haubrichs 1988

[154] On the relation of *Heldensage* and history see Schneider 1962, von See 1971, 61 ff, Gschwantler 1976; Haubrichs 1988

[155] Gschwantler 1976, 1979

parts of medieval Europe, available to any interested author for any purpose. When one examines particular *Heldensage* texts, the effects are immediately apparent. Often, where cross-referencing with other types of historical source is possible, a text centuries removed from contemporaneity will be found to have preserved more or less accurate historical information. At other times the information, though still recognisable as historically based, is garbled to some degree. At still other times the narratives are self-evidently unhistorical: anachronism, conflation of distinct narratives for literary effect, fabulous elements such as monsters and dragons, and so on. The consequence is that information offered by a *Heldensage* text which is neither self-evidently unhistorical nor verifiable with reference to some independent reliable source is of indeterminate value, however much one wishes it to be true.

Despite all this, as noted at the start of the current subsection, there is good reason to think that the information which the three poems offer is both relevant to and reliable for Anglo Saxon England. Two arguments are offered in support:

- Internal evidence from *Widsið*

    This first argument has to do with a tense-change in *Widsið:* the poet Widsið speaks in the past tense about his travels through the length and breadth of the migration-age Germanic world, but the narrator speaks in the present. When is the narrator's present? It is a commonplace of literary interpretation that narrators are not necessarily identical to authors, as any reader of Chaucer knows. A narrator can be a character manipulated for literary effect like any other. But 'not necessarily' means exactly what it says: narrator and author may be identical. Which is it here? If the narrator is indeed a character invented by the author of *Widsið* for some literary effect, then one would expect to be able to discover that effect, that is, to see why the author needed a buffer between himself and the reader, and how he used that buffer for some literary purpose. I can, however, see no such manipulation of the narrator, and no reason not to collapse narrator into author, making the narrator's present identical to the author's: Anglo Saxon England between c.700 and c.1000AD. On this interpretation, *Widsið* constitutes contemporary evidence for poets like Widsið among the Anglo-Saxons; because there is little in *Beowulf* and *Deor* which is not also explicitly or implicitly in *Widsið*, this means that the information which these three poems provide about court poets and their poetry applies directly to Anglo-Saxon England.

- The function of *Deor* and *Widsið*

Secondly, what were *Widsið* and *Deor* for? They are not narratives like *Beowulf* and the Old English biblical poems, nor are they Christian meditations like *The Dream of the Rood* or *The Wanderer*. Both are about the careers of court poets, and both end with appeals for patronage. Many decades ago W.H. French (1945) argued that these poems are in fact what they appear to be: *curricula vitae* presented to prospective patrons by actual court poets. This offers an elegant and economical explanation of the two poems, and it is presumably for this reason that French's proposal has been largely ignored ever since[156]. Literary interpretation being what it is, no definitive conclusion is possible, but seen from French's point of view the poems would have great authority on the subject of court poets and poetry in Anglo-Saxon England because they would have been composed by actual *scopas*.

Both arguments are based on the principle that the simplest empirically-justifiable reading of any given text is to be preferred, and can be regarded as an application of Occam's Razor[157] to interpretation of the two poems. This does not, of course, render the arguments conclusive, either individually or in combination, but it does

---

[156] For example Malone 1962; Eliason 1966; Howlett 1974. Discussion in Moisl 1979, 239 ff.
[157] Blackburn 1994, 268

constitute a coherent case for the relevance and reliability of the three poems' evidence on court poets to Anglo-Saxon England.

The remaining Anglo-Saxon documentation[158]

The discussion in this section is focussed on the following passage from one of the *Lives* of the East Anglian king Ethelbert, who was assassinated by Offa of Mercia in 794AD[159]. It is part of the account of Ethelbert's journey to Offa's court[160]:

> *Then, rendered cheerful, the holy king Ethelbert said: 'May the name of the Lord be blessed now and forever'. And he added: 'It often gladdens travellers when poems are recited to musical accompaniment. Therefore I will give an arm-ring to whomever can recite royal songs'. Immediately, two skilled in the art of song began to make music in gladness of heart. They were songs about the royal line of that same king Delighted by them, he took an arm-ring from his arm and bestowed it on those who had performed the songs, and promised more on returning home.*

This looks very much like the scenario derived from the poetic texts --poets in the royal retinue singing songs about kings, and more particularly about their patron's ancestors, and being rewarded for it by lavish gifts of treasure-- and given that it is about a demonstrably historical king of the later eighth century, would appear to corroborate a large part of what the poetic sources tell us for Anglo-Saxon England. Inevitably, however, there are serious problems with the *Life* as an historical document. It survives in a twelfth-century manuscript and, though there was arguably a pre-Conquest source, it is far removed from contemporaneity. Moreover, hagiography is not biography in the modern sense, and one might reasonably argue that Ethelbert was assimilated to a traditional *Heldensage*

---

[158] Much of this material is discussed in Richter 1994, ch. 6
[159] Yorke 1990, ch. 4
[160] James 1917, 238; passage discussed in Opland (1980b), 148 ff

kingship stereotype during the interval between his death and the composition of the version of the *Life* which survives. In short, the passage cannot be used to corroborate the poetic texts because it could easily have been influenced by the genre to which these texts belong. If, however, a good case could be made for the historical reliability of the passage, it would have substantial corroborative value. The rest of this section therefore attempts to make such a case by looking for evidence that the (i) court poets and (ii) royal dynastic historical tradition mentioned in the passage existed in Anglo-Saxon England.

Anglo-Saxon court poets

There are fairly numerous references to Anglo-Saxon secular poets, and more particularly court poets, from the later seventh century onwards. These are exhaustively collected and discussed by Opland[161]; only a representative selection is cited here. The earliest reference comes from the enactments of a council held in Rome in 679 AD, which concerned itself with the affairs of the English Church. It cautions *that bishops or those who have professed the religious life of ecclesiastical orders should not use weapons, nor should they have singers who accompany themselves to the harp, nor should they allow before themselves any jests or games*[162]. Writing in the early twelfth century, William of Malmesbury says that the great scholar Aldhelm was at about that same time exploiting secular minstrelsy as a preaching medium[163]:

> *Besides being fully conversant with Latin learning, he did not neglect songs in the native tongue, to the extent that, as the book of King Alfred of which I spoke previously attests, no one at any time surpassed him. He could make English poetry, compose songs, and either recite or sing them as appropriate... The holy man Aldhelm used to position himself in the way of those leaving the church on*

---

[161] 1980b, chapters 6 - 8
[162] Haddan and Stubbs 1871, 133
[163] Hamilton 1870, 336

the bridge which linked the monastery and the countryside, and
pretend to be a minstrel. He was from the beginning rewarded with
a favourable response and crowds. By this device, gradually
inserting words of scripture into the secular subject matter, he
brought the people to wholesomeness.

The Synod of Clofesho (755 AD) again found it necessary to stipulate *that*
monasteries be what their name implies, that is, virtuous dwellings of the silent,
the peaceful, and workers for God, and not receptacles for the mirthful arts, that
is, of poets, harpers, musicians, and low entertainers. Another of the canons in
the same collection specifies that *priests should not chatter in church like secular*
poets.[164]. And at the end of the eighth century comes what must be the most
quoted non-poetic passage in the study of Old English literature --Alcuin's letter
to Hygbald of Lindisfarne in 797AD[165]:

When priests dine together let the words of God be read. It is
fitting on such occasions to listen to a lector, not to a harpist, to
the discourses of the Fathers, not to the songs of the heathens.
What has Ingeld to do with Christ? Narrow is the house: it cannot
hold them both. The king of heaven will have no part with so-called
kings who are heathen and damned, for one king reigns eternally in
heaven while the other, the heathen, is damned and groans in hell.
In your houses the voices of the lectors should be heard, not a
rabble of those who make merry in the streets.

At Athelstan's coronation feast in 925AD, according to William of Malmesbury[166]:
The nobles assemble and place the crown. . . the palace seeths and
overflows with royal splendour. Wine foams everywhere, the great
hall resounds with tumult, pages scurry to and fro, servers speed

---

[164] Haddan and Stubbs 1871, 369 and 366
[165] Dümmler 1895, 183; see comments in Richter 1994 ch. 5, who also cites similar Carolingian references
[166] Stubbs 1887-9, 145-6; on William as historian see Thomson 1987, ch. 2

on their tasks; stomachs are filled with delicacies, minds with song.
One makes the harp resound, another contends with praises... The
king drinks in this honour with eager gaze, gaciously bestowing
due courtesy on all.

There are also various references in Old English poems apart from *Beowulf,*
Widsið, and *Deor* to poets and poetry in court contexts[167]. A central metaphor in
The Seafarer, for example, is the distinction between the rigors of the sea and the
comfortable life of the retainer in the court; on the sea *he has no thought for*
harping or receiving of rings[168]. Similarly, recalling happy times in the court, the
Riming Poem says[169]: *The warriors were keen; clear was the harp, it sang loudly;*
the laughter resounded. The Fortunes of Men lists a variety of skills possessed by
men who have had good fortune in life --the warrior, the scholar, the goldsmith,
and so on. Another of these skilled and fortunate occupations is this[170]:

> *One must sit at his lord's feet with the harp, receive payment, and*
> *always rapidly pluck the strings, let the plectrum that darts around*
> *produce sounds, the resounding nail.*

The canon collections and Alcuin's letter can be accorded considerable intrinsic
credibility. Why would a synod or a scholar of Alcuin's stature invent secular
poets in ecclesiastical contexts as straw men to knock down? It seems reasonable
to regard them as responses to perceived abuses in the Church. We can,
therefore, be confident that secular poets who recited poems about kings of the
past --Alcuin's Ingeld-- existed in Anglo-Saxon England at least until the end of
the eighth century. Moreover, Wormald has stressed the early secularisation of the
Anglo-Saxon Church[171] --that the Church had from the outset been assimilated to
the norms of the secular aristocracy which endowed, administered, and to a large

---

[167] These are collected in Opland 1980b, ch.8
[168] Krapp & Dobbie 1936, 144, line 44
[169] Krapp & Dobbie 1936, 167, lines 27-8
[170] Krapp and Dobbie 1936, 156, lines 80-83; there are similar passages in *Christ* (lines 664-85) and *The Gifts of Men* (lines 49-50)
[171] Wormald 1978

extent owned it. In particular, the hall of a seventh or eighth-century monastery would often have differed little from that of a secular aristocratic court; Bede, and later Alcuin, were much given to criticism of this tendency, and the above-quoted passage from Alcuin's letter to Hygbald is part of a much longer diabtribe against abuses of this sort at Lindisfarne. If poets and harpists sang in eighth-century monastic halls, and if these halls are a fair reflection of contemporary secular court life, then the conclusion must be that such performers were also active in contemporary secular courts.

The passage from William of Malmesbury, though late, is based on an Alfredian source, and William spent his whole life at the monastery of which Aldhelm was abbot in the seventh century[172], and so his sources are authoritative. The passage therefore usefully supports the conclusion just drawn on the basis of the early canon collections and Alcuin's letter.

The references from *The Seafarer* and the *Riming Poem* together with the Athelstan account are less straightforward. With Old English poetry there is constant uncertainty about the relationship between the text and contemporary reality. Given some feature --here, the presence of harpers in aristocratic courts-- does that feature correspond to contemporary reality, or is it an artefact of poetic tradition which describes something that may or may not have existed at some time in the past? This uncertainty extends to the Athelstan account. It locates praise poets in Athelstan's early tenth-century royal court. The text in which it is embedded, however, is an extravagantly literary Latin poem of uncertain provenance quoted by William, and does not necessarily describe the actual event. It could just as well be an assimilation to the literary *Heldensage* tradition which, as we know from the *Beowulf* manuscript and the *Exeter Book,* was current in the tenth and eleventh centuries in a way already suggested for the *Life of Ethelbert* passage. Despite the general problem of using Old English poetry as an historical source, however, there is good reason to believe the passage from *The Fortunes*

---

[172] Keynes & Lapidge 1983, ch. 24, 88-9; also 268; Thomson 1987

of Men. It belongs to a genre of 'poems of wisdom and learning'[173] which make gnomic observations on Life in general, and on Anglo-Saxon life in particular. There is no more reason to doubt the existence of the harper it describes than there is to doubt the existence of warriors, scholars, and goldsmiths at whatever time the poem in its current form was composed, and that harper played before a lord and received payment for it, just as the poets in the *Life of Ethelbert* did. The problem is that the poem is not reliably dateable beyond the observation that it occurs in the *Exeter Book* of c.1000AD, and hence cannot help us locate its harper chronologically.

Before assessing the corroborative value of these various references for the *Life of Ethelbert*, a final problem has to be dealt with. In many of them, the *poetae* and *citharistae* are associated with popular entertainment, and seem very different from the aristocratic *scop* of the poetic texts. There are also Old English and Old High German glosses of the tenth and later centuries linking *scop* and its cognate *scopf / scof* with such words as *comicus* and *ioculator*[174]. All this has occasioned a fair amount of discussion about the relationship between the *scop* of the Old English poetic sources --the aristocratic court poet or *Hofsänger*-- and the tradition of popular entertainment that extended from the Roman *mimus* and *ioculator* to *the jongleur* and *spilman* of the central and later middle ages[175]. Heusler[176], for example, thought that the Germanic peoples had in the course of their centuries-long interaction with the Roman Empire evolved an entertainer patterned on the *mimus,* who then developed into the aristocratic *Hofsänger,* only to return by the time of the glosses just mentioned to his lowly origins. For Baesecke[177], the *Hofsänger* stems from Germanic antiquity, but is in a state of decline by the time of the earliest medieval written records; when the glosses appear, he has already degenerated into a common entertainer. Most recently,

---

[173] Shippey 1976
[174] Wissmann 1954; Werlich 1967, 361-2
[175] Ogilivie 1963; Richter 1994, ch. 5 and 242 ff
[176] Heusler 1911, 445 and 460-62; also 1941, 113-23
[177] Baesecke 1941

Opland[178] has argued for a distinction between the *scop,* 'the tribal poet, a vatic soothsayer originally related to the sacral king, whose tradition weakens and probably atrophies during the eighth and ninth centuries, but might have enjoyed a late revival as a result of the activity of Scandinavian skalds', and the *gleoman* 'the (wandering) harper whose function is entertainment, who is a popular figure in monasteries and market places, and who, when associated with the scurrilous itinerant jugglers and actors, merits the consistent censure of the clerical hierarchy'. These two figures, according to Opland, 'were originally distinct, though some merging of the traditions might have taken place during the eighth and ninth centuries, when the tribal poet's status declined'. Such reconstructions seem to me radically underdetermined by the available evidence, but there is no need to assess their historical validity here because the relationship between popular entertainers and such court poets as there might have been is irrelevant for present purposes. What does concern us is the assumption that the Clofesho canons and the Alcuin passage, and material like them, refer to popular entertainers. If they do, then they cannot serve as evidence for the existence in Anglo-Saxon England of court poets like those of the poetic texts. That assumption is unjustified, however. The fact that Alcuin is scathing about *'rabble who make merry in the streets'* does not necessarily mean that the intended poets and harpists really were rabble, whatever that might mean. This passage, like those of the Roman synod, the Clofesho canons, and the above-mentioned glosses, has to be interpreted in the light of the Church's official intolerance of secular values and practices in ecclesiastical contexts[179]: the fact that ecclesiastical sources bracket *poetae* with popular entertainers does not necessarily imply a status lower than that of the *Hofsänger* in the poetic sources.

The material cited in this section shows beyond reasonable doubt that Anglo-Saxon secular poets performed in aristocratic courts as well as in monastic

---

[178] 1980b, 190
[179] Werlich 1967, 365; Wormald 1978; Richter 1994, ch. 5

halls, that one aspect of this performance was traditional material about kings of the past, that these poets were rewarded by their aristocratic patrons, and that they were active at least until the end of the eighth century. This corroborates some aspects of the *Life of Ethelbert* passage but says nothing about the poets' recitation of royal dynastic history. To this we now turn.

Royal dynastic tradition

This section first of all considers evidence that two Anglo-Saxon royal families, the Kentish and the Mercian/East Anglian, had dynastic traditions associated with them, and then goes on to argue that this was true of the other main dynasties as well.

Near the beginning of the early-eighth century *Life of St. Guthlac,* the saint's father is described as a man *from a distinguished line among the Mercians...The descent of this man ran in set order through the most noble and ancient names of illustrious kings from the beginning in Icel*; in the Mercian genealogy which survives as part of the the Anglian collection, Icel is the progenitor of the Mercian royal dynasty[180]. The *Life* goes on to say that Guthlac was inspired to take up the warrior's life appropriate to a young man of his descent *remembering the mighty deeds of ancient heroes,* but after a time *when he contemplated the miserable deaths by shameful end of the ancient kings of his race in past ages,* he gave it up and turned to religion[181]. Guthlac was not inspired to action and remorse by anything like the bare list of names which constitutes the approximately-contemporary Mercian genealogy, but by the tales of kings and heroes in his line of descent. The *Life* is dated c.730-40 AD, and Guthlac's reiving days must have been in the late seventh century[182]. One can, therefore, be certain that a body of historical tradition relating to the Mercian royal dynasty, or at least to a branch of it, existed at the turn of the seventh century, and that it was

---

[180] Dumville 1976
[181] Colgrave 1956, 72-4 and 80-82
[182] Colgrave 1956, 2-4 and 15-19

accessible to illiterate young dynasts who saw it as something relevant to their careers.

A fragment of Kentish dynastic history is actually extant. The story of the invasion of Britain by Hengest and his brother Horsa is simultaneously an account of the beginning of the Saxon kingdom of Kent, and of the establishment of its royal dynasty by Hengest. It appears in a variety of pre- and post-Conquest texts. Of the pre-Conquest versions --Gildas' *De Excidio Britonum*, Bede's *Ecclesiastical History*, the *Historia Brittonum*, the *Anglo-Saxon Chronicle*, and the *Chronicle of Æthelweard*-- the most fully developed is that of the *Historia Brittonum* (dated c.830 AD)[183], and what follows is based on it.

The *Historia Brittonum* says that Hengest and Horsa were exiled from Germany and that, having arrived in Britain, they were given an island to live on and a promise of maintenance by the British king Vortigern for their help against the Britons' enemies. The Saxons agreed, but after a time they grew burdensome to their hosts and were asked to leave. Hengest's response was to send home for reinforcements. He then prepared a feast and invited Vortigern. When Vortigern saw Hengest's daughter he was so besotted that he offered Hengest half his kingdom in exchange for her. Hengest settled for Kent, and assuring Vortigern that he would be ever more zealous in defending the British against their enemies, he continued to gather Saxon reinforcements in Kent. At this point the narrative breaks off and there is some intervening unrelated material. When the narrative resumes, we find Vortigern's son Vortimer engaged in a series of battles against the Saxons. At first he succeeds in driving them back, and even manages to kill Horsa, but then Vortimer himself dies. Vortigern now invites the Saxons back and a peace conference is arranged. Both sides agree to come unarmed, but the Saxons devise a plot to hide knives in their boots, and at the signal *'nimað sexa'* -- the Old English words actually appear in the text-- to kill everyone but Vortigern. This happens as planned. Vortigern is ransomed for Essex and Sussex, and the

---

[183] Dumville 1985, sections 19-20, 24-27; on Nennius see Field 1996

Saxon numbers in Britain grow. On Hengest's death his son Octha succeeds *and from him all the kings of Kent to the present day are descended.*

The occurrence of the expression *nimað sexa* is one of several criteria that Chadwick, (whose discussion of this material remains fundamental[184]) used to demonstrate that the *Historia Brittonum* version of the account is ultimately based on an English source. His further conclusion, that the source was Kentish, follows naturally. The clause also indicates that this Kentish source was in the vernacular[185]; extensive plot development and use of direct speech further suggest that that vernacular source was *Heldensage* poetry, as does Hengest's betrayal of a kinsman by marriage, a motif strongly reminiscent of the conflicts of loyalty so often found in Germanic *Heldensage*[186].

The case for thinking that all the major Anglo-Saxon dynasties had traditions of the above sort associated with them rests mainly on the extant corpus of royal genealogies, but also receives some support from evidence that oral traditions about the various dynasties were extant throughout the Anglo-Saxon period.

The genealogies are lists tracing the descent of Bernician, Deiran, East Anglian, Mercian, East Saxon, West Saxon, and Kentish kings from legendary and mythical ancestors. The eighth-century Anglian collection[187] and the early ninth-century *Historia Brittonum*[188] contain the most comprehensive collections, but individual genealogies also occur in greater or lesser degrees of elaboration in various other texts such as Bede's *Ecclesiastical History* and the *Anglo-Saxon Chronicle*.

As extant, these lists are products of ecclesiastical scholarship[189]. But was the keeping of genealogical records an innovation brought about by Christian

---

[184] Chadwick 1907, 35-53. See also discussions by Moisl 1981 and Brooks 1989
[185] Moisl 1981; Brooks 1989; Yorke 1990, 3
[186] Schneider 1962
[187] Dumville 1976
[188] Dumville 1985
[189] Sisam 1953

literacy, or an originally native, pre-Christian genre which the Church adapted? Early scholarship tended to favour the nativist position[190]. More recently there was a tendency to be sceptical about any Germanic precedent, though the arguments have been far from conclusive[191]. There is, however, a case for thinking that the lists are as a group based on pre-existing royal dynastic tradition, and opinion is moving that way again[192].

The genealogies standardly draw descent from pagan gods: in the East Saxon case it is Seaxnet, also attested as a god of the continental Saxons[193], and in all the others it is Woden. Contemporaries were well aware that these were names of pagan gods. If confirmation is needed, one can turn to the *Historia Brittonum* which, having followed descent beyond Woden to Geta, observes that Geta *was, they say, the son of a god, not of the true, all-powerful God. ..but one of their idols*[194]. On the one hand, descent from a pagan god is naturally explicable as an aspect of pre-Christian Anglo-Saxon belief. Moreover, divine descent is attested for three of the Germanic peoples we have looked at so far -- Suebi, Ostrogoths, and Franks-- and, as a letter from Daniel, Bishop of Winchester to Boniface between 722 and 732 AD shows, *the genealogy of false gods* was at that time an aspect of pagan Germanic mythology[195]. On the other hand, there is no obvious motivation for churchmen to invent such a piece of pagan mythology, especially since the Church had by the period with which we are here dealing evolved its own theory about the relationship between the Christian God and secular authority, and it had nothing to do with Woden[196]. The element of descent from a pagan god in the genealogies must be based on a pre-Christian belief about royalty. Now, we have seen the evidence for the existence of Mercian and

---

[190] Chambers 1959, 316-17
[191] Sisam 1953; Dumville 1977, 96, 100, 102
[192] Moisl 1981; Brooks 1989, Yorke 1990, 15-16
[193] Yorke 1985
[194] Dumville 1985; also Asser's *Life of Alfred,* (Stevenson (1904)), ch. 1: *...which Geta the pagans venerate as a god*
[195] Tangl 1916, nr.23
[196] Ullmann 1966

Kentish dynastic traditions at about the time the genealogies were compiled. It seems inconceivable that the compiler(s) of the lists would have ignored existing dynastic traditions and created wholly new lines of descent, complete with a piece of pagan mythology, especially since, as we know from the *Life of St. Guthlac*, dynasts were well aware of their families' histories. And, in fact, the Kentish history and the corresponding genealogical list agree in the early stages of descent. The indication is that the Anglo-Saxon royal genealogies were based on pre-existing traditions associated with the major Anglo-Saxon royal dynasties.

Support for the existence of dynastic traditions comes from ecclesiastical texts which, there is reason to believe, drew on orally-transmitted material relating to the dynasties in question. This type of evidence was also available for the Goths, the Lombards, and the Franks, but was relegated to a supporting role because of the subjectivity involved in deciding, usually on stylistic grounds, what was and what was not based on an oral source. The same reservation applies to the corresponding Anglo-Saxon material[197]. Historiographers work with the evidence they have, and we know that Anglo-Saxon historiographers used oral tradition. William of Malmesbury actually says in his *Gesta Regum*[198] that he got his information about the earlier period of Anglo-Saxon history *more from old songs popular through succeeding ages than from books written for the instruction of posterity,* and much of his text has stylistic features consistent with such a source. So, for example, do Bede's story of Eomer attempting to assassinate the Northumbrian king Edwin[199] and his account of Oswiu's murder of Oswine[200], or, for Wessex, the saga of Cynewulf and Cyneheard in the Anglo-Saxon Chronicle for the year 755 AD[201]; it is tempting to construe the *English poems* which Alfred heard *frequently...recited by others* in the court, and

---

[197] Collected by Wright 1939 and Wilson 1970
[198] Stubbs 1887-9, 1, 155
[199] Colgrave & Mynors 1969, II.9
[200] Colgrave & Mynors 1969, III.14
[201] Bately 1986, 36

which he held in such esteem that he committed them to memory[202], as the West Saxon equivalent of Guthlac's family traditions, but there is no indication in Asser's text about the nature of these poems. The trouble with material of this sort is that, even assuming agreement on an oral source, it is insufficiently focussed for present purposes in that one cannot in general decide whether it originates in specifically dynastic traditions of the kind being posited here. The most one can say is that such material is consistent with such traditions.

Returning now to the passage from the *Life of Ethelbert*, how plausible is it in the light of the other evidence presented in this section? The *Life* shows poets travelling with the royal retinue, and being generously rewarded for their performance. The other evidence establishes the existence of secular and more particularly court poets up to the end of the eighth century. The *Life* has the poets reciting dynastic history before the king. The other evidence confirms the existence of vernacular dynastic traditions for two major Anglo-Saxon dynasties, and provides a reasonable basis for thinking that other dynasties too had such traditions attached to them. The link which the *Life of Ethelbert* makes between court poets and dynastic tradition is, however, not supported by the other evidence.

Poetic and non-poetic evidence combined

It remains to integrate the categories of evidence discussed in (a) and (b) above. Both (a) and (b) agree on the existence of Anglo-Saxon secular and more specifically court poets; (a) does not provide chronological location in the period, but (b) guarantees their existence at least to the end of the eighth century. The two categories also agree that these poets cultivated historical and more specifically royal dynastic tradition. The poet's status in the court, his role as panegyricist, and the role of panegyric in the generation of historical tradition all depend on the intrinsic credibility of (a), however.

---

[202] Stevenson 1904, chapters 22, 76; see commentary in Keynes & Lapidge 1983

iii. Lordship and historical tradition among the Anglo-Saxons

The poetic sources indicate that panegyric was a medium for the political exploitation of historical tradition. Panegyric celebrated *dom,* and that *dom* was a necessary basis for kingship was lost to no one in *Beowulf:* the greater an individual's *dom,* the more suited he was to be king. Beowulf himself considered that, in performing deeds which brought him *dom,* he was demonstrating his qualification for lordship. Telling Hygelac of his adventures in Denmark, he says that he went after Grendel's mother *to display my lordship, risk my life, do a glorious deed* (2131 -34). His contemporaries agree. After achieving *dom* for killing Grendel, *Beowulf's fame was proclaimed; many repeatedly declared that nowhere in the wide world was there a shield bearer more noble than he under the expanse of the heavens, more worthy of a kingdom* (857-61). Hroþgar begins his famous speech to Beowulf after the slaying of Grendel's mother with: *Your glory, Beowulf my friend, is exalted throughout distant regions. . . You shall become a comfort to your people, a help to heroes* (703-05), and continues with a lengthy disquisition on the qualities that ought and ought not to characterise a ruler. The obvious implication of all this is made explicit in Hroþgar's farewell speech to Beowulf (1845-53):

> *I think it likely, if it comes about that the spear...should take Hreþel's offspring Hygelac, king of the Geatas, your chief, the guardian of the nation, that the Sea-Geatas would have no better man to choose as king and guardian of the treasure hoard of heroes, if you wish to hold your kinsman's kingdom.*

Hroþgar also sends with Beowulf the visible tokens of his *dom* --the treasure given him for his bravery. On returning home Beowulf presents Hygelac with it, and thereby in effect with the evidence of the qualifications for lordship which he has acquired. Hygelac's response is to award him a symbol of lordship --the sword which formerly belonged to Hreþel-- and a vast estate over which Beowulf can rule (2144-99). And, when he eventually attains the kingship of all the Geatas, Beowulf strives to manifest his lordship by maintaining his *dom,* the reputation for valour which had made him king. In undertaking to attack the dragon, he wants *to achieve a famous deed* and win *dom,* but in the same breath makes clear that he can thereby *display lordship* (2510-47).

In celebrating Beowulf's *dom,* therefore, the *scop* was not only realising the hero's commitment to lasting personal glory, but also advertising his eligibility for lordship. The narrator in *Widsið,* in offering poetry to the patron *who wishes to display his dom before the troop, to manifest his lordship,* was doing the same. But one measure of Beowulf's *dom* was his similarity to a great hero of the past: historical tradition is here being applied to Beowulf's political advantage; a case has been made for the existence of court poets like those who appear in *Beowulf, Widsið, and Deor,* and thereby for the role of panegyric in the political application of historical tradition, in Anglo-Saxon England.

The above argument is important because it portrays the political exploitation of historical tradition in a quintessentially non-literate, barbarian context. It is based on slender evidence, however. We turn now to supporting evidence.

Pagan gods as progenitors of royal dynasties were not merely a picturesque remnant of the past in Anglo-Saxon England, but a politically significant feature of dynastic legitimacy. Referring to Ida, whom the genealogies reckon as the progenitor of all branches of the Bernician dynasty, the tenth-century *Chronicle of Æthelweard* explains the significance of descent from a pagan god as follows: *Ida...whose line of descent takes the beginning of its royal authority and of its nobility from Woden*[203].

But it was genealogy in general, not just the element of divine descent, which served to legitimize authority. The *Parker Manuscript*[204] in the

---

[203] Campbell 1962, 12

[204] On what follows see Parkes 1976; see also comments by Dumville 1989, 123-5

mid-tenth century contained (i) the genealogy of the West Saxon royal house down to Alfred, (ii) the *Anglo-Saxon Chronicle* to 925 AD, with its heavy emphasis on the achievements of the West Saxon kings, and (iii) the laws of kings Ine and Alfred of Wessex: 'It suggests a conscious attempt on the part of this compiler, active some time during or after the reign of Athelstan, to preserve the tradition of the West Saxon royal house in its purest form'[205], and closely resembles what Charlemagne and Rothari had done with their law codes earlier.

There are, moreover, indications that the genealogies were manipulated so as to give a dynastic basis to contemporary political circumstances[206]. As already noted, all the dynasties for which genealogies are extant, with the exception of the East Saxon one, are derived from Woden. Those of Mercia, Lindsey, and East Anglia descend independently from different sons of the god, but Wessex and Bernicia, and Kent and Deira, are jointly descended from two more sons, Baeldæg and Wægdæg respectively. Dumville makes a good case for thinking that descent from Woden was not original to Kent and Wessex, but was an innovation reflecting dynastic relationships between them and the northern kingdoms of Deira and Bernicia --'that the inclusion of Kent and Wessex in the Anglian collection expresses their inclusion in the eighth century within the Anglian world. In other words...descent from Woden expresses an Anglian origin, or perhaps - more cautiously-- belief in an Anglian origin'[207]. Support comes from the fact that names from the Bernician line of descent make up the generations between Woden and Cerdic in the West Saxon genealogy. All this begs the question of how many other royal families may have been incorporated into the scheme. The occurrence of Seaxnet at the head of the East Saxon line indicates that there was once a variety of founder gods; one may with de Vries and Turville-Petre want to see the names Hengest and Horsa as cult names, and significance in the fact that the name of Hengest's son Oisc, from whom the Kentish family descended, represents

---

[205] Parkes 1976, 167
[206] Dumville 1977
[207] Dumville 1977, 79

Germanic *anskiz, a nominative singular i-stem formation from the root ans-, 'god', otherwise attested, for example, in the ansis from whom the Ostrogothic Amal dynasty drew its descent[208].

---

[208] Moisl 1981, 235-6; Brooks 1989, 59

3. THE CELTS

Historical overview[209]

As with the Germans, 'Celts' is here used not in a political or ethnic sense, but rather to designate those barbarian European groups who spoke dialects of Indo-European classified as Celtic on linguistic grounds, or who were dominated by Celtic-speaking lords. There is not the same historical sensitivity about 'Celt' as there is for 'German'. Nevertheless, a well established Celtomania does exist, and the intent of the proposed definition is to dissociate this study from romantic notions of celticity transcending time, space, and politics.

The Celts emerged as an identifiable culture in central Europe about the middle of the first millennium BC. From about that time they began to extend their area of influence not only into territories on the periphery of their central European core, but also into more distant regions. There were Celts in Iberia by the mid-fifth century BC, and also in the Po valley of northern Italy, from where they raided southwards and even sacked Rome in 387 BC. To the east, Celts are attested in Thrace in the mid-fourth century BC, and soon thereafter began raiding in Greece itself. They even managed to establish a Celtic kingdom in Galatia, which bears their name. The progress of expansion northwards is obscure, but by the first century BC present-day northern France, Belgium, and Britain were thoroughly Celtic. By the end of the third century BC, the Celts were the dominant culture of central and western Europe. Thereafter, however, their fortunes were to decline.

In the east, raiding in Thrace and Greece had not resulted in any stable domains, and the Celts soon lost their ethnic identity and disappeared from history; the Galatian kingdom managed to survive to the end of the second century BC, when it was brought to an end by the kings of Pergamum. In the

---

[209] This section is based on Cunliffe 1979, 1988; Beresford Ellis 1990; Green 1995; Birkhan 1997

west, the decline was mainly a consequence of the extension of Roman control northwards. The Celts of the Po valley suffered a succession of military defeats which led in turn to Roman colonisation of their territories, the offer of Roman citizenship, and finally incorporation, as Cisalpine Gaul, into the Roman federation. The Iberian Celts had allied themselves with Carthage during the Punic Wars of the third century BC and were, after the Roman triumph, subjected to a process of pacification which brought them under Roman domination by about 100 BC. The subjugation of the Celtic heartland began with the increasing Roman influence in the areas around Massalia, and then northwards to the Pyrenees and Narbonne in the late second century AD; between 58 and 51 BC, Julius Caesar singlehandedly extended Roman control over the whole of Gaul by a series of military campaigns. Caesar also made an attempt on Britain. It was unsuccessful, but between 43 and 84 AD Britain, too, was incorporated into the Empire. In all these conquered territories there were greater or lesser degrees of romanisation, depending mainly on geography: the Celts of Gallia Narbonensis to the south were already heavily romanised when Caesar began his conquest, but in the far north and west the influence was weaker. Everywhere, though, the Celtic ethnic consciousness waned and eventually disappeared, and from the fourth century AD any remnants were overlaid by Germanic migrants. The only Celtic areas to have remained outside Roman domination and later Germanic settlement, and thus to have retained and developed their Celtic culture without major interference, were geographically peripheral ones: Ireland, the parts of Britain corresponding to present-day Scotland, Wales, and Cornwall, and the north-west corner of Gaul.

102

a) GAUL[210]

The history of Celtic Gaul pivots on the campaigns of Julius Caesar between 58 and 51 BC. The details of why and how Caesar managed to subjugate so many Celtic tribes over so large an area in so short a time are not important for this discussion. The effects are, however, and simply put they are as follows. Before 58 BC the Celts of Gaul had had a way of life which Graeco-Roman observers perceived as ethnically distinctive. After 51 BC, the process of assimilation to characteristically Roman social, political, and economic institutions progressively superseded the Celtic ones, to the extent that, by the end of the first century AD, the original Celtic culture was gone. This is, of course, too simply put. Pre-Caesarean Celtic culture did not develop in splendid isolation. There is plenty of evidence, beginning about 600 BC, for extensive trading contacts with the mediterranean world via Massalia and similar ports which grew up subsequently. Southern Gaul was, moreover, already heavily romanised on the eve of Caesar's campaigns; indeed, it was ostensibly to support one such romanised tribe, the Aedui, that Caesar went into Gaul in the first place. Nor, in the century and a half after Caesar's campaigns, was romanisation uniform either geographically or across social classes. In core areas of Gaul, however, old tribal areas were redefined as Roman administrative units, many tribal *oppida* became cities, and the old aristocracy became Roman citizens and administrators. Schools for the children of the Celtic aristocracy were established, and Latin was increasingly used by the ruling class. There were Celtic institutional survivals, mainly in rural or remote areas, and the Celtic language continued to be used into the third and fourth centuries in some places, but the essence of pre-Caesarean Celtic culture was gone.

---

[210] Drinkwater (1983); Cunliffle 1979, 1988; Beresford Ellis 1990;Birkhan 1997

i. Gaulish lordship[211]

Most of what is known about Gaulish lordship comes from Caesar's *Gallic War*. Caesar fought with Gaulish lords, negotiated with them, and even came to know some of them personally over the space of nearly a decade. He was consequently in a unique position to comment on Gaulish political structure and politics, and he often did. One might want to argue[212] that the early-to-mid first century BC was a particularly fraught time for Gaul, with Germans to the east and Romans to the south, and that Gaulish lordship then was not necessarily as it had been earlier. That may well be true, but as it happens the evidence for Gaulish historical tradition relates precisely to this time, and the snapshot of Gaulish lordship which Caesar provides is just what we need.

Caesar includes an ethnographical excursus in the *Gallic War*[213], part of which is a general account of Celtic social and political structures. On social structure he has the following to say[214]:

> *Throughout Gaul there are two classes of persons of definite account and dignity. As for the common folk, they are treated almost as slaves... The greater part of them, oppressed as they are either by debt or by the heavy weight of tribute or by the wrongdoing of more powerful men, commit themselves in slavery to the nobles...Of the two classes mentioned above one consists of the druids* ('druides') *and the other of the nobles* ('equites')...*At the onset of war --and before Caesar's coming this would happen virtually every year, in the sense that they would be making wanton attacks themselves or repelling such-- the equites all take part. Each has dependents and clients* ('clientes') *about him in*

---

[211] For a useful discussion of Gaulish political institutions see Cunliffe 1988, 92 ff and 117 ff; Birkhan 1997, 986 ff

[212] Cunliffe (1979), 140-41

[213] Seel 1961, VI.11-28

[214] Seel 1961, VI.13

104

proportion to his birth and resources, and this is the one form of influence and power known to them.

Gaulish society was dominated by a warrior aristocracy whose *influence and power* --on which more below-- was based on *dependents and clients* which noble birth and wealth were able to attract. In another passage of the ethnography Caesar expands on the political ramifications of the clientage system[215]:

> *In Gaul, not only in every tribe* ('civitas') *but also in every country district* ('pagus') *and region* ('pars'), *there are factions* ('factiones'). *The leaders* ('principes') *of these factions are men who in the judgment of their fellows are deemed to have the highest authority, men to whose decision and judgment the supreme issue of all cases and counsels may be referred. These seems to have been the arrangement from ancient days, to the end that no man of the people should lack assistance against a more powerful neighbour, for each man refuses to allow his own folk to be oppressed and defrauded; otherwise he has no authority among them. The same principle holds throughout Gaul...*

Civitas is the word that Caesar uses consistently in referring to what he saw as the primary political groupings of Gaul; by his reckoning there were 46 of them. As the above passage suggests, a *pagus* is a subdivision of a *civitas:* the *civitas* of the Helvetii, for example, *is divided into four pagi*[216]. Permanent political groupings larger than the *civitas* are nowhere mentioned, though temporary alliances between and among *civitates* were frequent.

In a general commentary on the political scene in Celtic Britain at the start of the Roman invasion in 43 AD, Tacitus writes that *in former times they owed obedience to kings, but now they are torn by party factions between rival leaders*[217]. This perfectly describes the scene that Caesar describes throughout the

---

[215] Seel 1961, VI.15
[216] Seel 1961, I/12
[217] Ogilvie 1967, ch. 11

Gallic War. Dominating political life, both within the *civitas* and in relations among *civitates*, was a warrior aristocracy whose members were constantly competing for what Caesar variously calls *regnum* and *imperium* --that is, sovereignty within the *civitas*, over groups of *civitates* and, occasionally and fleetingly, over the whole of Gaul. The success with which an aristocrat could vie for *regnum* depended crucially on his ability to attract *clientes*, less powerful aristocrats as well as commoners, who promised military and economic support in exchange for protection against other predatory lords. If successful, he could emerge as the *princeps* of *a factio* which constituted his political power base. The struggle for *regnum* and *imperium* among *principes* created a chronic state of actual or impending war within and between *civitates*. Aversion to any institutionally permanent lordship appears to have been universal.

The following example is typical of many others in the *Gallic War*. The Helvetii were a *civitas* in present-day Switzerland: *Among the Helvetii the most noble man by far, and the richest, was Orgetorix*[218]. This Orgetorix was *possessed of a desire for regnum,* and therefore *persuaded the community to march out of their territory in full force, urging that as they excelled all in valour it was easy enough for them to secure imperium over the whole of Gaul.* He also recruited allies from outside his own *civitas.* One of these was Casticus, *son of the Catamantaloedes who had for many years held regnum over the Sequani,* whom he urged *to seize in his own civitas the regnum which his father had held before him.* The other was Dumnorix, a *princeps* of the Aedui who, by various subterfuges, *increased his own property and acquired ample resources for bribery; he maintained a considerable body of horse at his own expense, and kept them about his person.* Dumnorix had *gained great favour among the people on account of his generosity,* and so *his authority extended over a large part of the population;* when Caesar arrived in Gaul, Dumnorix *had achieved principatum in the civitas, and had the allegiance of a large part of the people.* He too was

---

[218] For what follows see Seel 1961, I/2-4, 9, 26

urged by Orgetorix to seize the *regnum*. Indeed, said Orgetorix, he was about to do that very thing in his own *civitas*. *There was no doubt,* he observed, *that the Helvetii were the most powerful tribe in the whole of Gaul, and he gave them a pledge that he would win them their own kingdoms with his resources and his army.* Moreover, having sworn an alliance, the three *hoped that when they seized regnum they would be able, through the efforts of the three most powerful and steadfast civitates, to master the whole of Gaul.* When the other Helvetian *principes* got wind of this plan, however, they summoned Orgetorix for trial. *On the day appointed for his trial, Orgetorix gathered all his people from every quarter to the place of judgment, to the number of some 10,000 men, and also assembled all his debtors and clients, of whom he had a great number.* Incensed, the other *principes* undertook *to secure their rights by force of arms,* and, as they were gathering their own forces, Orgetorix died under suspicious circumstances. As for Dumnorix, the other Aeduan *principes* appealed to Caesar for help against his growing power within the *civitas,* and after several unheeded warnings Caesar had him assassinated.

Among the Aedui the ban on individuals claiming *regnum* had been institutionalised in the office of the *vergobretus*[219]. At one point, Caesar called together the Aeduan *principes,* two of whom were Diviciacus and Liscus, *who held the highest office, which the Aedui called vergobretus, to which they appointed every year and which had the power of life and death among them*[220]. This reference to the *vergobretus* is supplemented later in the *Gallic War* when the *principes* of the Aedui come to Caesar *with a matter of utmost importance to the civitas. The civitas was in the greatest danger because, having long ago agreed to appoint a single office with royal authority each year, two contenders were vying for the office, both claiming that they were entitled to it by law*[221]; one

---

[219] Le Roux 1959; Wolfram 1975, 272 ff
[220] Seel 1961, I/16
[221] Seel 1961, I/18

candidate's brother had been *vergobretus* the year before, and was therefore disqualified because *the law forbade two members of the family from holding the office in a single generation.* This *vergobretus,* therefore, yields what Caesar regards as *regiam potestatem,* 'royal power', but only for a short fixed term, and without being able to pass it on in the family, and is clearly a sort of constitutional monarch appropriate to a situation in which the ambition and power of the *equites* within the Aeduan *civitas* demanded a mechanism to balance their claims.

ii. Gaulish historical tradition

<u>The sources</u>

The writings of Greek and Roman authors provide the earliest documentation relating to the Celts. There are brief references from the sixth century BC, but for present purposes they become interesting only from the second century BC onwards, and are at their most informative both in terms of quantity and quality of information offered in the first century BC and the first AD[222]. Because of the increasing romanisation of the Celtic areas of Europe after this time, later texts which mention the Celts tend to draw on existing literary sources rather than on direct observation or report for their --now less expansive-- material; after the fourth century AD even these derivative sources of information slow to a trickle and then disappear. Thereafter the Celts drop out of history until texts originating in the fringe Celtic areas begin to appear in the early medieval centuries.

The main Graeco-Roman sources for Gaulish historical tradition are[223]:

1. Diodorus Siculus (c.90 - 30 BC)
2. Strabo (63 BC - 21 AD)
3. Livy (59 BC - 17 AD)
4. Lucan (39 - 65 AD)

---

[222] For general commentary on Classical references to the Celts see Tierney 1960; Chadwick 1966; Nash 1979; Rankin 1995

[223] Dates are taken from Hammond & Scullard 1970

5. Dio Chrysostom (40 -115 AD)

6. Appian (active c. 100 AD)

7. Athenaeus (active c.200 AD)

8. Claudius Aelianus (c. 170 - 235 AD)

9. Ammianus Marcellinus (c.330 - 391 AD)

The chief difficulty in using these sources is that Classical authors were bound neither by copyright laws nor by the standards of modern scholarship. They borrowed freely and eclectically from existing sources, sometimes with acknowledgment but most often without, and felt free to interweave their own direct experience or incidental knowledge. This presents self-evident problems with regard to the provenance and reliability of the information which the above eight authors provide, and exemplifies the difficulties set out in the Introduction. In 1960 Tierney[224] made a bold attempt to impose order on the chaos of extant ethnographical material relating to the Celts of Antiquity. Posidonius, a Greek historian, is known to have written a history of the Roman wars fought in southern Gaul during the late second century BC, and to have included a Celtic ethnography in it. That history, written c.80 BC, is no longer extant, but parts of it survive in extracts included by other writers in their own work. Tierney proposed a reconstruction of Posidonius' lost ethnography, arguing that the four authors on which we depend for the bulk of our information about Gaulish Celtic institutions --Julius Caesar, Diodorus Siculus, Strabo, and Athenaeus-- borrowed most or all of what they wrote about the Celts from Posidonius, and that 'there is very little ethnographic material in later writings on the Celts which does not come from the four authors mentioned, and ultimately from Posidonius'. This, if true, would simplify the situation radically. There would be only one substantial primary Classical source on the Celts; its author Posidonius is known to have travelled in

---

[224] Tierney 1960

southern Gaul and thus to have had an opportunity of observing the Celts personally.

That Diodorus Siculus, Strabo, and Athenaeus depend chiefly on Posidonius has been generally accepted, but the rest of the reconstruction has not. In particular, Caesar has been re-established as a primary source essentially independent of Posidonius[225]. The derivation of Tierney's 'later writings' from the same Posidonian source was, moreover, asserted rather than demonstrated, and in fact appears incapable of demonstration. No doubt many, perhaps even most, of these later writers knew and used Posidonius and Caesar, but they could also have had access to other information whose provenance is unknown.

The evidence

As with the Anglo-Saxons, the evidence for historical tradition and its relation to lordship among the Gauls is inextricably tied to the court poet's role as custodian of that tradition. The Gaulish court poet was closely associated with the well organised and politically influential priestly-learned order of druids[226]. Caesar writes that *throughout Gaul there are two classes of person of definite account of dignity...Of the two classes one consists of druids* ('druides') *and the other of nobles* ('equites')[227], thereby equating the druids in terms of social status with the ruling aristocracy of Gaul. Other writers claim that the druids exercised substantial influence over these lords. Dio Chrysostom writes that, *since they cannot always be ruled by kings who are philosophers, the most powerful nations have publicly appointed philosophers as superintendents and officers for their kings,* and cites Persian magi, Egyptian priests, and Indian brahmans as examples; he goes on: *The Celts appointed those whom they call druids, these also being devoted to the prophetic art and to wisdom in general...In all these cases the kings were not*

---

[225] Nash 1979

[226] There is a voluminous literature on the druids, most of it nonsense. Good recent accounts are Beresford Ellis 1994; Ross 1995; Birkhan 1997, 896 ff

[227] Seel 1961, VI.13

permitted to do or plan anything without the assistance of these wise men, so that in truth it was they who ruled, while the kings became their servants and the ministers of their will, though they sat on golden thrones, dwelt in great houses, and feasted sumptuously[228]. The provenance of Dio's information is unknown, and there is clearly a philosophical agenda here --the doctrine of the philosopher-king[229]-- not to speak of rhetorical overstatement. But confirmation that there is a core of truth here comes from Caesar's description of his dealings with one particular *civitas*, the Aedui, and in particular with a certain Diviciacus. Cicero tells us that Diviciacus was a druid: *Nor is the practice of divination disregarded even among uncivilised tribes, if indeed there are druids in Gaul -- and there are, for I knew one of them myself-- Diviciacus the Aeduan, your guest and eulogist. He claimed to have that knowledge of nature which the Greeks call 'physiologia' and he used to make predictions, sometimes by means of augury and sometimes by means of conjecture*[230]. This is the same Diviciacus who has already been mentioned as one of the two persons holding the Aeduan office of *vergobretus*, and who was deeply involved in Caesar's political manoeuverings in Gaul. Caesar also indicates that druidical involvement in religious ritual had a political application when he writes that *sacrifices of this kind are also traditionally offered for the needs of the state*[231].

The the above citations indicate, the druids' influence was based on their learning and priestly functions: they were *philosophers, devoted to the prophetic art and to wisdom in general,* had *knowledge of nature which the Greeks call 'physiologia', used to make predictions, sometimes by means of augury and sometimes by means of conjecture,* and offered sacrifices *for the needs of the state.* Caesar goes into greater detail not only about the nature of this knowledge, but also about how it was maintained both in terms of training and of the way in

---

[228] Crosby & Cohoon 1949-61, vol.4, 301
[229] Hammond & Scullard 1970
[230] Falconer1946, XLI.90
[231] Seel 1961, VI.13

which the druidical order was organised[232]:

The former [that is, the druids]...*are concerned with divine worship, the due performance of sacrifices, public and private, and the interpretation of ritual questions. A great number of young men gather about them for the sake of instruction and hold them in great honour. In fact it is they who decide in almost all disputes, public and private; and if any crime has been committed, or murder done, or there is any dispute about succession, they also decide it, determining rewards and penalities...Of all these druids one is chief, who has the highest authority among them. At his death, any other who is pre-eminent in position succeeds, or, if there be several of equal standing, they strive for primacy by a vote of the druids, or sometimes even with armed force. These druids, at a certain time of the year, meet within the borders of the Carnutes, whose territory is reckoned as the centre of Gaul, and sit in conclave at a consecrated spot. Thither assemble from every side all that have disputes, and they obey the decisions and judgments of the druids...Report says that in the schools of the druides they learn by heart a great number of verses, and therefore some persons remain twenty years under training And they do not think it proper to commit these utterances to writing... The cardinal doctrine which they seek to teach is that souls do not die, but after death pass from one to another...Besides this, they have many discussions touching on the stars and their movement, the size of the universe and of the earth, the order of nature, the strength and power of the immortal gods, and hand down their lore to the young men...The whole nation of the Gauls is greatly devoted to ritual observances, and for that reason those who are smitten by the more grievous maladies and who are*

---

[232] Seel 1961, VI.13

engaged in the perils of battle either sacrifice human victims or vow to
do so, employing the druids as ministers for such sacrifices

According to Caesar, then, the druids (i) were a priesthood, (ii) were organised in the sense that there was a hierarchy of authority within the order and a system of educating recruits, (iii) cultivated a body of orally transmitted tradition which ranged over mythology, law, and natural philosophy of sorts, and (iv) were socially influential by virtue of their learning in that they oversaw religious ritual and administered justice. Did they also cultivate specifically historical tradition of the sort which has interested this study thus far? Caesar notes that *the Gauls all assert their descent from Dis Pater, and say that this is the druidic belief*, which resembles the claim to descent from Tuisto which Tacitus attributes to his Germans, but to go any further one has to look beyond Caesar's *Gallic War*.

Writers in the Posidonian tradition broadly agree with Caesar's comments on the druids, but make a distinction of interest which Caesar does not make; Strabo writes[233]:

> *Among all the tribes, generally speaking, there are three classes*
> *of men held in special honour: the bards, the seers ('vates'), and*
> *the druids. The bards are singers and poets, the vates interpreters*
> *of sacrifice and natural philosophers, while the druids, in*
> *addition to the science of nature, study also moral philosophy.*

That is, the Posidonian tradition allocates the competence which Caesar attributes to the druids to separate functional groups. We shall be primarily interested in the bard. Does the druids' politically influential position extend to the bard? There has been a good deal of discussion about the interrelationship of druid, *vates*, and bard in the literature, and about the significance of Caesar's failure to make the distinction, but it is inconclusive. It may be, for example, that the bard's function as singer and poet was an aspect of general druidical competence, in which case

---

[233] Jones 1917-32, IV.3 19

the answer is yes, but the Posidonian separation of functions could well reflect a hierarchy. All one can say is that the druidical order was politically influential by virtue of its learning, and that the Posidonian tradition associates the bard with that order.

Texts in the Posidonian tradition describe the bards as a class of poets who euologised members of the aristocracy in return for their patronage, and who cultivated historical traditions about their patrons' ancestors. Strabo describes the bards as *singers and poets,* as we have seen. Athenaeus gives a brief and somewhat garbled account of the context in which such poets functioned[234]:

> *The Celts have in their company, in war as well as in peace,*
> *companions whom they call parasites. These men pronounce their*
> *praises before the whole assembly and before each of the chieftains*
> *in turn as they listen. Their entertainers are called bards. These*
> *are poets who deliver eulogies in song.*

Athenaeus has misunderstood Posidonius here[235]. The *parasites* and bards are one and the same, the former being a term to describe their dependence on the chieftains' patronage. Athenaeus elsewhere supports this with the observation that the bards *pronounced praises* in aristocratic assemblies[236], as does Diodorus Siculus, who notes that *the lyric poets whom they call bards...sing to the accompaniment of instruments resembling lyres, sometimes a eulogy and sometimes a satire*[237]. What was eulogised? For the answer we turn to Appian, who describes an expedition led by Gnaeus Domitius against the Allobroges, a Celtic *civitas,* in 121 BC[238]:

> *When he was passing through the territory of the Salyi an*
> *ambassador of Bituitus, the king of the Allobroges, met him*
> *magnificently arrayed and followed by attendants...A musician,*

---

[234] Gulick 1927, VI.49
[235] Caerwyn Williams 1979-80 for another view of these 'parasites'
[236] Gulick 1927, VI.49
[237] Oldfather 1933-67, V.31
[238] White 1912, I.115

too, was in the train, who sang in barbarous fashion the praises of King Bituitus, and then of the Allobroges, and finally of the ambassador himself, celebrating his birth, his bravery, and his wealth. It is for this reason chiefly that ambassadors of distinction take such persons along with them.

In addition to citing *birth, bravery, and wealth* as criteria for eulogy, this passage supports Athenaeus in locating the court poet in the lord's retinue. And, in return for eulogy, the bard was generously rewarded, as the following passage from Athenaeus shows[239]:

Posidonius again, when telling of the wealth of Louernius, the father of the Bituitus who was dethroned by the Romans, says that in an attempt to win popular favour he rode in a chariot over the plains distributing gold and silver to the tens of thousands of Celts who followed him. Moreover, he made a square enclosure one and a half miles each way, within which he filled vats with expensive liquor and prepared so great a quantity of food that for many days all who wished could enter and enjoy the feast, which was being served without break by attendants. And when at length he fixed a day for the end of the feast, a Celtic poet who arrived too late met Louernius and composed a song magnifying his greatness and lamenting his own late arrival. Louernius was very pleased and threw a bag of gold to the poet, who was running alongside the chariot. The poet picked it up and sang another song saying that the very tracks made by his chariot on the earth gave gold and largesse to mankind.

In addition to such eulogy, the bard cultivated historical tradition which propagated the memory of great men through successive generations. Claudius Aelianus, commenting on the Celts' general ferocity, writes: *The Celts above all*

---

[239] Gulick 1927, IV.37

men love danger. They take as the themes of their songs those men who have met fine deaths in battle[240]. Such songs were the preserve of bards in particular. Ammianus Marcellinus says that *the bards sang of the mighty deeds of famous men in heroic songs to the lovely tune of the harp*[241], and Lucan writes of *the bards...who by the praises of their verse transmit to distant ages the fame of heroes slain in battle*[242].

There are no Gaulish examples of historical tradition as there are for the Anglo-Saxons, but there is some reason to believe that one Classical writer, Livy, drew on Gaulish such tradition for some of his material. The most likely candidate for borrowing of this sort is an origin legend very like those of the Germanic peoples already discussed. Livy introduces it with the words *Concerning the migration of the Gauls into Italy, we are told as follows. . .* , which may indicate a vernacular source; he continues[243]:

> *The Celts, who make up one of the three divisions of Gaul, were under the dominion of the Bituriges, and this tribe supplied the Celtic nation with a king. Ambigatus was then the man, and his talents together with his arms and general good fortune had brought him great distinction; for Gaul under his sway grew so rich in corn and so populous that the immense multitude looked as though it would soon become hard to rule. So the king, being old and wishing to relieve his kingdom of its excess population, declared that he would send his sister's sons, Bellovesos and Sigovesos, who were energetic youths, to whatever country the gods should indicate by omen, and that they could take as many men as*

---

[240] Dilts 1974, II.31
[241] Rolfe1935, I.178-80
[242] Barratt 1979, I.440 ff
[243] Foster 1919, V.24

they wished, so that no people should be able to resist their
advance. The omens assigned the Hercynian forest to Sigovesos,
and to the more fortunate Bellovesos the road to Italy.

Livy's source could well have been the Romano-Celtic writer Cornelius Nepos (c. 100 - 25 BC)[244], a native of Cisalpine Gaul, or Trogus Pompeius[245], another Celtic writer working at about the same time, though there is no certainty about either. Nor is any putative Celtic source for this passage assured, and it is here used only in a supporting role for the other evidence about Celtic vernacular historical tradition cited above. The same goes for the bewildering variety of Celtic origin accounts which Ammianus Marcellinus offers, one of which he claims to have *read...inscribed upon their monuments*[246].

iii. Lordship and historical tradition among the Gauls

Diodorus Siculus at one point in his ethnography describes the Gaulish aristocracy's preparations for battle. It includes the following:

It is also their custom, when formed in battle, to step out in front of
the line and to challenge the most valiant man from among their
opponents to single combat, brandishing their weapons in front of
them to terrify their adversaries. And when any man accepts the
challenge to battle they break forth into a song in praise of the valiant
deeds of their ancestors and in boast of their own high achievements,
all the while reviling and belittling their opponent and trying by such
talk to strip him of his bold spirit before the combat.

Gaulish aristocrats knew songs about their family histories, and valued them as indicators of status alongside their own personal qualities. We have seen that bards were custodians of historical tradition. It seems reasonable to infer that, when one such bard celebrated his patron, the aristocrat Bituitus, in terms *of*

---

[244] Hubert 1932, 148-9
[245] Beresford Ellis 1990, 23
[246] Rolfe 1935, XV/9

his birth, his bravery, and his wealth, his songs made reference to Bituitus' family history. In the same passage Appian furthermore comments that *it is for this reason chiefly that ambassadors of distinction take such persons along with them.* Dynastic historical tradition was, therefore, used by Gaulish aristocrats as a criterion of status, and the bard applied that criterion by public recitation of panegyric verse.

b) IRELAND[247]

Irish history before the later fifth century AD is largely obscure. The Romans never incorporated Ireland into the Empire, and the Germans never invaded it, so it remained generally unnoticed and undocumented apart from a few brief and not very informative references in Graeco-Roman texts[248]. Only with the arrival of organised Christianity and literacy[249] in the fifth and sixth centuries does Ireland truly emerge from prehistory. By the time Christianity arrived, Ireland was predominantly Celtic in the sense that the ruling class spoke a Celtic language. When and how these Celts came to Ireland is, however, far from clear. True, there are clues. Some of the numerous surviving Irish vernacular texts of the period before about 1200 AD describe successive waves of migration into Ireland[250], and others a world uncannily similar to that of the Gaulish Celts described by Caesar and Posidonius[251], but at the same time archaeology has so far provided strangely little support for such a culture in Ireland[252]. There is also a wealth of Irish place-names, study of which might yield some insight into settlement patterns. It may eventually be possible to integrate such clues with archaeological evidence to arrive at a coherent and plausible reconstruction of the earliest knowable phase of Irish history, but the current state of research is still some way from that[253].

Fortunately, the obscurity of pre-fifth century Irish history is not a problem for this discussion. In accordance with the methodology outlined in the Introduction, assumptions about a Celtic ethnicity common to Ireland and pre-Caesarean Gaul need not be and are not made. The available Irish documentation in part describes Ireland in the early post-Conversion centuries and in part allows

---

[247] This section is based on Mac Niocaill 1972; Byrne 1973; Harbison 1988; Richter 1988; O Croinin 1995

[248] Beresford Ellis 1990, 180; O Croinin 1995, 14 ff

[249] O Croinin 1995, ch. 7

[250] Byrne 1973, 9 ff; McCone 1990, ch. 3

[251] Jackson 1964. See also McCone 1990 and O Croinin 1995, 45 ff

[252] Raftery 1984; Harbison 1988, esp. 166 ff; Mytum 1992, 22

[253] Harbison 1988; Mytum 1992; O Croinin 1995, chapter 1; Birkhan 1997, 386 ff

some plausible extrapolation into the pre-Christian period, and it is treated purely as such.

i. **Irish lordship**[254]

Ireland at the start of the historical period was divided into numerous, in principle independent groups which were the building blocks of early Irish polity. The Old Irish word for such a group was *tuath*, which is normally translated as 'tribe' but is more accurately described as 'a population group which formed a distinct political entity'[255]. The *túath* was dominated by an aristocracy centred on a kingship which was the hereditary prerogative of a royal family. Governing relations between king and aristocracy, and between both of these and freemen commoners, was a system of clientage whereby an individual bound himself to a lord, and thereby established a relationship involving reciprocal obligations: what the lord offered was essentially protection and finance, and the client service in kind, return on the finance, and allegiance in times of war. The number and relative social level of a lord's clients determined his wealth, his status, and his political influence. This system produced a pyramidal hierarchy within the *túath* whereby the king at the apex had his clients as members of the higher aristocracy, each of whom had his own clients drawn from a lower level, and so on down to the level of freemen clients.

The clientage system could and did extend beyond the *túath*. Depending on his resources at any given time, the king of a *túath* might attach himself to some more powerful king, and/or might himself be lord of one or more less powerful colleagues. This produced a pyramidal hierarchy or *túatha* (plural of *túath)* as a continuation of the one within each *túath,* at whose apex was the *rí ruirech,* the 'king of over-kings'.

---

[254] This section is based on O Corrain 1972; Mac Niocaill 1972; Byrne 1973; Charles-Edwards 1988; McCone (1990), chs. 5-6; O Croinin 1995, chapters 3 and 5
[255] Byrne 1973, 8

This tidy political structure emerges primarily from the Irish laws, which are by nature systematic and normative. Nothing in real life is as neat as lawyers would like it to be, and the picture that emerges from other sources is rather more turbulent. For one thing, there is a tendency from the earliest period for major dynasties to dominate their less powerful subordinates, and even to intrude their own candidates into the subordinates' royal succession, with a consequent erosion of the status of petty kings and of the independence of individual *túatha*. For another, the texts of the Ulster Cycle --early Irish *Heldensage*, of which more later-- depicts an Ireland strikingly like the Gaul which Posidonius and Caesar describe, and gives some idea of the character of the Irish ruling class in prehistory: the king Conchobor mac Nessa presides over a retinue of professional warriors devoted to the standard heroic dictum 'death or glory', and is in an endemic state of war with similarly oriented and constituted courts of 'the men of Ireland'. When written annals take us out of prehistory and allow us to observe Irish lordship more directly, hardly a year goes by without at least one battle being recorded, the causes of which are various --lords executing obligations from recalcitrant clients, clients trying to throw off oppressive lords, boundary disputes between *túatha*, royal succession disputes, power struggles between branches of royal dynasties, major wars between the provinces into which Ireland was divided by the start of the historical period: Ulster, Leinster, Munster, Connacht, and Meath. One can, of course, easily overstate the martial aspect of Irish lordship. No society can be at war most or even much of the time and still survive. There are children to be raised, crops to be cultivated, farms to be tended, and the aristocracy must have spent most of its time doing these things. The Ulster Cycle is literature, not history, and there is little literary capital in efficient agricultural management; annals record notable events, not the normal routine of everyday life. Nevertheless, these sources do capture a real aspect of Irish kingship in the early medieval centuries.

ii. **Irish historical tradition**

The sources[256]

The discussion has so far tried to glean every scrap of evidence for the existence and exploitation of historical tradition among each of the groups it has dealt with, from the early Germans through to the Gauls. For Ireland, the problem is just the opposite[257]. The corpus of early medieval documentation relevant to the subject of this study is very large, both absolutely and in comparison to what exists for the other groups, and there is no alternative but to be selective, though care has been taken to make the selection a representative sample of what is available.

An overview of the texts to be used is given below. Some preliminary methodological observations are necessary, however.

- All the texts in the early Irish vernacular corpus were 'undoubtedly produced either in monasteries or by people who had received an essentially monastic education'[258].

- The texts can be classified according to their temporal reference: (i) those which explicitly or implicitly refer to a reality more or less contemporary with the time of writing, and (ii) those which refer to a distant, usually pre-Christian past.

- These two classes present different problems of historical interpretation. For class (i) one must come to a judgment on the reliability of what any given text claims for its contemporary reality using a combination of source criticism and, where possible, corroborative method. For class (ii), judgment of authoritativeness with respect to any reality, past or present, on the basis of source criticism is generally intractable, as already noted with reference to Germanic *Heldensage*. As with *Heldensage*, at least some of the content of class (ii) texts derives from oral tradition with roots in prehistory. Oral tradition

---

[256] McCone 1989, 1990 for a general discussion of the genesis of the vernacular corpus
[257] See the comments of O Croinin 1995, 8
[258] McCone 1990, 1

can accurately preserve information over long periods[259], but just because it *can* gives no guarantee that it always *does*, and there is no obvious way of knowing when it does and when it doesn't. The literary redaction of orally transmitted material was, moreover, not always and probably not even very often a matter of mouth to hand transcription. The days when one could believe in monastic scribes committing oral traditions to writing as accurately as possible for the benefit of posterity, perhaps with the odd scrap of piety thown in, are long gone. As a rule, such traditions were given literary form for a reason, and that implies interpretation rather than simple transcription, which in turn implies innovation both to the form and content of the orally transmitted material. And, once oral traditions have been given literary form, there is always the possibility a --usually unknown-- sequence of recensions preceding the extant text.   One can never be sure whether an extant noncontemporary text preserves historically reliable information about the past via some line of oral and/or textual transmission now lost, or projects contemporary reality onto the past, or invents the past wholesale, or combines all these things in some proportion[260]. The only way to validate the information they provide is to corroborate it.

The two classes of text need to be distinguished in what follows. For convenience, category (i) texts are henceforth referred to as 'contemporary', and category (ii) as 'non-contemporary'. Some texts combine contemporary and non-contemporary reference; such cases are pointed out as required in the course of discussion.

- Textual dating

As far as I am aware, all the texts used here date from the Old Irish and Middle Irish periods, which are conventionally taken to cover c.700 - c.900 AD and c.900 - c.1200 AD respectively. Most can be assigned to one or another of

---

[259] Vansina 1985
[260] McCone 1990, ch. I

the two periods, typically on orthographical and linguistic grounds, and some can be more narrowly dated to particular centuries or parts of centuries, but few can be assigned specific dates. Fortunately, this level of imprecision in textual dating is not a problem for us. The aim of the book as a whole is to study the interaction of lordship and tradition in barbarian Europe, and, as the Introduction notes, this is taken to mean before c.1000 AD. For present purposes it is sufficient to demonstrate such an interaction for Ireland prior to that date; greater chronological precision, where available, is of course desirable, but is nevertheless a bonus.

Most of the material referred to in what follows is encompassed by five textual categories: annals, laws, metrical tracts, genealogies, and prose sagas. Occasional reference is made to texts which do not belong to any of these categories; these are described as they occur.

Annals[261]

There is evidence for the keeping of contemporary records of important Irish events from the later sixth century onwards. From the mid-seventh, a contemporary set of annals based on such records was established and thenceforth maintained in Iona. In the mid-eighth century a copy of this Iona chronicle was brought to the Irish mainland, and this became the basis for several different sets of annals which were thereafter continued year by year for many centuries. In these annals, therefore, we have a contemporary record of Irish events from the mid-seventh century, and a good case can be made for the reliability of some entries as far back as the later sixth, though the possibility of interpolation and/or revision must always be borne in mind.

---

[261] Smyth 1972; Mac Niocaill 1975; Grabowski & Dumville 1984; Dumville 1985b; Moisl 1987; Aitchison 1994, 34 ff

Secular laws[262]

The surviving corpus of Irish secular law is very extensive. It is in the vernacular, and contains textual strata of varying dates. The oldest, so-called 'canonical' stratum was written down between about the mid-seventh and mid-eighth centuries, and is based on law which was orally transmitted in the form of mnemonic verse, examples of which are quoted in the surviving tracts[263]. This earliest stratum is literally surrounded in the manuscripts by extensive commentary dating from the Old and Middle Irish and on into the Early Modern Irish (c.1200-c.1500 AD) periods. Much of the commentary is mere speculation on the meaning of the canonical stratum, but some of it does reveal later innovations to the law and not infrequently contains quotations from early texts which no longer survive.

Much has been made of the conservatism of early Irish law[264] --of the proposition that it represents legal traditions more relevant to conditions obtaining in a distant past than to contemporary reality-- but recent scholarship has come to regard that proposition as exaggerated[265]. On the one hand, we shall see that there was a legal profession in Ireland throughout the period up to c.1000 AD, and it seems natural to assume that the body of law with which this legal profession coexisted had something to do with its work. On the other, the surviving tracts show that a major new element in Irish society, the Church, was comprehensively incorporated into traditional legal structures, and both the form and content of the tracts show strong influence from ecclesiastical canon law and Christian ideology[266]. Both these things indicate that the law was subject to revision by its

---

[262] Most recently on the laws see Breatnach 1984, 1987, 1988, 1996; Charles-Edwards (1980, 1993, 3ff); Kelly 1988; McCone 1990, ch. 4; O Corrain 1984a, 1987; O Croinin 1995, 122 ff; the standard edition is Binchy 1978
[263] McCone 1990, 41 ff
[264] For example Binchy 1943; discussion in O Croinin 1995, ch. 5
[265] O Corrain 1987; McCone 1989; McCone 1990, ch. 4
[266] Breatnach 1984; O Corrain 1984a, 1984b; McCone 1990, 25 ff; see also ch. 4; O Croinin 1995, 123 ff

custodians, and that it was intended by them to be broadly relevant to contemporary reality. The Church can in fact be observed using this law to further its aims[267]. In short, the law tracts can be taken to be contemporary texts, though with due caution[268]: conservatism remains a factor, and their pervasive schematisation of society must not be too literally interpreted.

Metrical tracts[269]

As their name implies, these texts are treatises on poetry, and more particularly on varieties of poetical metre. They are conventionally dated to the Middle Irish period, and like the laws are a working genre. Their format identifies them as textbooks which were probably used in the training of professional court poets, of whom more later. As such they can be taken to relate to contemporary reality in a fairly direct way.

Genealogies[270]

The genealogies trace the descent of Irish royal dynasties from legendary ancestors into the historical period. As a genre they are particularly liable to politically inspired manipulation. Indeed, it is a mistake to think of them primarily as records of biological history. They were a medium for political propaganda for which historical accuracy was simply irrelevant[271]. Fortunately, this does not compromise their value for us, since they will be used not to trace details of dynastic history, but rather to exemplify the role of royal or dynastic history *per se* in the legitimisation of lordship.

The discussion will deal with only one tract, that of the Laigin, the ruling dynasty of the province of Leinster. It contains two strata of different dates,

---

[267] Moisl 1987
[268] For example Charles-Edwards 1993, 3 ff
[269] Thurneysen 1891; for dating Thurneysen 1912, 78-89; Breatnach 1987, 58
[270] O'Brien 1962; O Corrain 1985; Charles-Edwards 1993, 111 ff; McCone 1990, ch. 10
[271] O Corrain 1972, 75 ff; Dumville 1977; McCone 1990, ch. 10; Charles-Edwards 1993, 111 ff;

126

denoted Leinster A (twelfth century) and Leinster B (tenth century)[272], and we will be interested primarily in Leinster A.

Prose sagas[273]

There are scores of vernacular prose sagas dating from Old Irish to Early Modern Irish times. Their subject matter is diverse; it is on the basis of subject matter that modern scholarship has categorised them into 'cycles'. Two of these cycles are important for present concerns:

- Ulster Cycle

  These tales centre on the royal court of the province of Ulster at Emain Macha, and deal with the chronic state of warfare which existed between Ulster and the rest of Ireland in pre-Christian times. The main Ulster protagonists are King Conchobor mac Nessa and the heroes of his court, chief among them Cú Chulainn. On the side of what the tales call 'the men of Ireland' are King Aillil and Queen Medb, who also have a court full of heroes at Cruachu in Connacht. The centre-piece of the Ulster Cycle is the epic *Táin Bó Cuailnge* ('The Cattle Raid of Cooley'), but there are numerous associated tales as well.

- King Cycle

  The tales of the King Cycle deal with the histories of major early medieval royal dynasties such as the Uí Néill, the Eóganachta, and the Connachta. In particular, they describe the foundation of these dynasties and the earliest stages of descent from the dynastic progenitor. In a few cases kings belonging to the Conversion and early post-Conversion period are referred to, but as a general rule the tales are concerned with pre-Christian Ireland.

---

[272] Charles-Edwards 1993, 177 ff
[273] Thurneysen 1921; Dillon 1958; MacEoin 1989; McCone 1990, ch. 8; Mallory & Stockman 1994

There is a close connection between the genealogies and the King Cycle. That connection will be important later on. For the moment, it is sufficient to note that the kings who feature in the tales are the same as the ones from whom the genealogical tracts draw the descent of royal dynasties: dynastic founders, their immediate descendants, progenitors of the main collateral branches. The fact that some king tales actually occur in the genealogical tracts, where they serve to elaborate on early stages of descent, shows that the genealogists regarded the tales as the historical foundation on which their own work was built.

The earliest manuscript versions of the prose sagas date from c.1100, but orthographical and linguistic criteria are routinely used to argue that these and later manuscript versions are either copies of earlier ones, or that they at least incorporate materials from earlier texts. Thurneysen's *Die irische Helden- und Königsage bis zum siebzehnten Jahrhundert*, published in 1921 and still the standard work on Irish prose sagas, takes the view that saga writing in Ireland began not much earlier than the eighth century, and this appears to remain the accepted view among specialists in early Irish literature[274]. As the title of Thurneysen's study indicates, moreover, the sagas continued to be written throughout the medieval and on into the early modern period. The world they depict is, however, overwhelmingly pre-Christian, and hence predates c.500 AD. Even the earliest of the sagas are therefore noncontemporary documents. For present purposes there is consequently no point in attempting to establish precise dates for the individual sagas referred to in what follows, since, as already noted, the historical accuracy of the information offered by noncontemporary texts cannot in general be established by source criticism. Put simply, a late text might preserve historically accurate information via some now-unknown line of transmission, and an early one might be pure invention; the only way of validating the information is via corroborative evidence. It is, therefore, taken as sufficient to observe that the

---

[274] McCone 1990, 180

sagas used here have all been dated by Thurneysen and their various editors to the Old and Middle Irish periods.

The evidence

The early post-Conversion centuries in Ireland saw the rise of a learned elite which was unique in dark-age Europe in that it was an amalgam of Christian monastic culture and of a priestly-learned order which had been a primary structural element in pre-Christian Irish society[275]. We are interested in the latter component of that elite. One of the functions of the priestly-learned order had been cultivation historical tradition, and as such its characteristics in general, and its relation to lordship in particular, are important for this discussion. The account which follows is in two main parts The first describes relevant aspects of the priestly-learned order as it appears in non-contemporary texts without attempting to assess their historicity, and the second corroborates as much of that description as possible using contemporary material.

The priestly-learned order in non-contemporary references

The pre-Christian Irish priestly-learned order[276] in non-contemporary sources had a variety of functions which can be divided into four broad categories. Firstly, it was a priesthood and professed the appropriate learning and skills: mythology, prophecy, and magic, together with the requisite rituals. Secondly, it maintained a corpus of legal learning. Thirdly, it cultivated historical tradition in general, and royal dynastic history more particularly. And fourthly, it composed panegyric verse for royal and aristocratic patrons. Members of the order were typically attached to royal courts, where they (1) serviced the cult of sacral kingship, (2) influenced the king's conduct by the prophetic and magical powers

---

[275] McCone 1990

[276] As already noted. there is a voluminous and largely useless literature on it. Good accounts are Caerwyn Williams 1971; McCone 1990, ch. 1;Beresford Ellis 1994; Ross 1995; Birkhan 1997, 896 ff. For the reconstruction which follows see Moisl 1987, Breatnach 1987, and Richter 1994, ch.8

which they claimed, (3) advised the king in his legal affairs and in matters involving royal judgment, (4) maintained dynastic tradition, and (5) praised the king on public occasions. We shall be looking at a selection of the evidence for each of these aspects. The order was also organised in the sense that it had a hierarchy based on a conjunction of seniority and competence, and a training discipline. These features are, however, peripheral to this discussion, and are not further developed in what follows.

A preliminary note on terminology. The texts use a variety of terms to refer to the priestly-learned order: *druí, fili, éces, fáith, brithem, bard*. In principle these terms refer to specific functions. The *druí* and the *fáith* are sacral; the *brithem* is legal; the *fili, éces*, and *bard* relate primarily to historical tradition and panegyric. There is overlap among them, however. The *fili* in particular is associated with all these functions.

In non-contemporary texts *druíd, filid*, and *brithemain* (plurals respectively of *druí, fili*, and *brithem*) are regularly portrayed as standard members of royal courts. Dozens of examples could be cited. One of these comes from the Ulster Cycle tale *The Conception of Cú Chulainn*, which evokes the archetypal heroic-age court of Conchobor mac Nessa. That court contains representatives of the main aristocratic estates of early Irish society: Fergus the warrior, Blaí Briugu the wealthy landowner, Cathbad the *druí*, Amargen the *fili*, Sencha the *brithem*[277]. A similar and demonstrably very early account can be found in Muirchú's later-seventh century *Life of St. Patrick*, which evokes the very epitome of the pagan Irish court at Tara which it was Patrick's mission to overcome[278]:

> *It so happened in that year that a feast of pagan worship was being held, which the pagans used to celebrate with many incantations and magic rites and other superstitious acts of idolatry. There assembled the kings, satraps, leaders, princes, and nobles of the*

---

[277] Van Hamel 1933, 20-21
[278] Bieler 1979, 85 ff; discussed in McCone 1990, ch. 3, 4

people; furthermore the magicians, fortune tellers, and inventors
and teachers of every craft and skill were also summoned to King
Loiguire at Tara...

These magicians and their like included two *druíd* and a *fili*, Dubthach maccu
Lugair[279].

• The sacral function

One of the ideas which the sources claim for pre-Christian Ireland was that
the pagan gods embodied the arts and crafts practised by humanity. The chief god
Lug *samildánach* ('uniting many crafts') appears among the Túatha Dé Danann, the
gods of pre-Christian Ireland, claiming mastery of all the arts and crafts[280]. One of
these arts is *druídecht*, 'druidism': *The Túatha Dé Danann were in the northern*
islands of the world learning wisdom (fis) *and sorcery and druidism* (druídecht)
and witchcraft and cunning until they surpassed the sages of the arts of
heathenism[281]. The god among the Túatha Dé Danann particularly associated with
druídecht was the Dagda. He says of himself: *I am Aed Abaid of Ess Rúaid, the*
good god of druídecht of the Túatha Dé Danann, and Rúad of Great Wisdom and
Eochaid the Great Father are my names[282]*;* of Rúad of Great Wisdom another
text notes: *It is he who had the perfection of heathen wisdom*[283].

The Ulster Cycle hero Cú Chulainn's claim that the *druí* Cathbad had tutored
him *in the arts of the god of druídecht*[284] epitomizes the divine origin of *druídecht*
and its investment in the human *druí*. Various texts describe or refer to
mythologies of divine inspiration in which *fís*, 'widsom', is channeled from the
Otherworld into this one. One example says that the river Boyne flows out of Síd
Nechtain, the *síde (*plural of *síd)* in general being being the domain of the pagan

---

[279] McCone 1986, 1990, ch. 4
[280] Stokes 1891a, 74 ff
[281] Stokes 1891a, 56
[282] Bergin 1927, 402
[283] Stokes 1897, 356
[284] Van Hamel 1933, 30

gods and Nechtan another name for the god Nuadu[285], and that its name inside the *síd* is Segais[286]:

> *This is a poem which Cormac mac Cuilennáin made concerning*
> *the remarkable nuts which fell from the hazel trees of Crimann,*
> *which surround Segais. Segais is the name of waters or of a well*
> *which is in Fir Breg...Into this well used to fall the nuts of these*
> *trees and thereafter into the Boyne every seventh year or every*
> *year until they came to various people, and the nuts were full of*
> *imbas, and they used to drink the imbas out of them.*[287]

The key word here is *imbas:* it comes from **imb-fis,* 'all-encompassing widsom'[288], which grows and matures in the Otherworld and, via the sacred river Boyne, is carried into the world of men.

This type of mythology finds its expression in ritual whereby the *druí* claimed access to Otherworld wisdom. Numerous texts use a standard formula for such druidical ritual: the *druí had recourse to his fis and his eólas* ('knowledge') in order to interpret some omen or to predict the future, and the desired interpretation *was revealed*[289], or *the gods to whom they sacrificed told them...*[290]. It included such things as sleeping on hurdles of rowan or on bull hides, *looking at their own images in water, or gazing at the clouds of heaven, or listening to the noise of the wind and the chattering of birds*[291], among many others[292].

Access to the Otherworld is held not only to confer prophetic but also magical powers on the *druí*. He can induce fertility in women[293] or delay birth[294],

---

[285] O'Rahilly 1946; de Vries 1961, 100ff

[286] O'Rahilly 1946, 318-23; Wagner 1975

[287] Thurneysen 1927, 268

[288] Thurneysen 1932, 163-4; Breatnach 1981; McCone 1990, 166-9

[289] Comyn & Dinneen 1902-14, viii, 348-50; Thurneysen 1921, 364-5; Dobbs 1923, 398; Fraser 1915, 19; MacSweeney 1904, 40-42; Sjoestedt 1926-7, 18; Carney 1940, 192; Best 1907, 154

[290] Dobbs 1923, 398

[291] Comyn & Dinneen 1902-14, viii, 348-50; also Dobs 1922, 8-10; Sjoestedt 1926-7, 28; O'Rahilly 1961, 142

[292] McCone 1990, ch. 7

[293] Stokes 1897, 392

[294] O'Brien 1962, 188-9

and cause forgetfulness[295]. Mountains are made to topple[296], or land to become infertile[297]. The *drui* can raise a river out of its bed[298], cause stormy seas[299], induce drought[300], or relieve it[301]. He can raise winds and mists which induce madness[302]. He can fly through the air[303] and change himself and others into animals and stones[304]. And, like prophecy, such powers came to the *drui* via ritual contact with the Otherworld. The *drui* Art, for example, *had recourse to his god* and, with his breath, caused a fog to form over a plain[305], and another, Colptha, *went to the pinnacle of his fis and his devilish eólas and had recourse to his god*[306].

Contact with the Otherworld and the powers which this conferred is in numerous texts shown to have given the *drui* considerable influence over kingship. The *drui* is standardly portrayed as an established member of the court who administered the royal cult, advised the king by virtue of his prophetic powers, and used his magic to the king's advantage. An adequate treatment of the first of these --his role as priest in the cult of royalty-- would involve a reasonably detailed account of Irish sacral kingship[307], which would take us too far afield. We will, however, consider the other aspects of the *drui*'s relationship with kings.

A good place to start is with two passages which capture the essence of the relationship between king and *drui* as it is portrayed in non-contemporary texts. The first comes from the Ulster Cycle tale *The Intoxication of the Ulstermen*. King Conchobor mac Nessa stands up during a feast: *The Ulstermen were silent when they saw the king standing. Such was their silence that if a needle fell from*

---

[295] Meyer 1910, 58
[296] Gray 1982, 43
[297] Plummer 1910, vol.1, 85
[298] Sjoestedt 1926-7, 31
[299] Macalister 1938-56, vol.5, 38, 54
[300] Sjeosetdt 1926-7, 50 ff
[301] Sjoestedt 1926-7, 74-6
[302] Sjoestedt 1926-7, 24-8, 32, 74, 86-8
[303] Sjoestedt 1926-7, 110
[304] O'Rahilly 1976, 30; Meyer 1901, 120; Sjoestedt 1926-7, 112
[305] Sjoestedt 1926-7, 36
[306] Sjoestedt 1926-7, 48
[307] Binchy 1970; Birkhan 1997, 882 ff

the roof to the floor you could have heard it. One of the taboos of the Ulstermen was to speak before their king, and one of the taboos of the king was to speak before his druids. Then Cathbad the druí said...[308]. The second episode occurs in *The Cattle Raid of Cooley*. Someone burst into the court at Emain Macha to say that heavy casualties were being inflicted on the Ulstermen in battle: *No one answered. It was a prohibition for the Ulstermen that any of them should speak before Conchobor, and Conchobor did not speak before his three druids. 'Who carries them off? Who drives them away? Who slays them?', asked a druí.* Explanations having been given, the *druí* goes on: *'It is right', said the druí, 'to kill the man who has disturbed the king'. 'It is fitting for him', said Conchobor. 'It is fitting for him', said the Ulstermen*[309]. In the second passage it is not only the outright statement of the *druí's* precedence that is significant, but also the sequence in which the decision to kill the messenger was made.

In *The Wooing of Ferb* Conchobor has a dream. He tells his wife about it, and she replies: *Go to Cathbad for advice about it...and take the advice which he gives you*[310]. This Conchobor does. Cathbad *druí* interprets the dream as portending victory for the Ulstermen, and that is indeed the outcome. This episode sums up a good part of the relationship between king and *druí* as the non-contemporary texts portray it: the *druí* advises the king on the basis of his prophetic knowledge, and the king acts on the advice to ensure success in his affairs. There are relatively few subjects on which the *druí is* shown to give advice, chief among them dynastic establishment and succession[311], fortune in war[312], and the circumstances of the king's own death[313].

The King Tale *Conall Corc and the Corco Luigde* puts the other main aspect of druidical influence over kingship with great economy: *King Óengus mac*

---

[308] Watson 1941, 10-11
[309] O'Rahilly 1976, 104
[310] Windisch 1897, 472
[311] For example Meyer 1901, 108; O'Brien 1962, 94-5; Hull 1931-4, 8; O'Daly 1975, 64; Dillon 1952, 67; Meyer 1907-13, 59
[312] Stokes 1903, 180; Sjoestedt 1926-7, 18-20; Meyer 1901, 116
[313] O'Brien 1962, 188-9; Stokes 1902, 422

Nad Froich had been routed in thirty battles until he met the drui Boinda. From then on he paid Boinda. In thirty battles he was victorious...[314]. Numerous other texts show *druid* accompanying their royal patron into battle and using various kinds of magic in furtherance of victory. In *The Battle of Mag Mucrama* King Eogan asks his *drui to satirize the enemy and chant against them*[315], and in the *First Battle of Mag Tuired their seers and wise men stationed themselves on pillars and points of vantage making their druidecht against the opposing army*[316]. What is accomplished emerges from the *Second Battle of Mag Tuired*, where a *drui* says of his contribution to an imminent battle[317]:

> *Three showers of fire will be rained upon the faces of the Fomorian host, and I will take out of them two-thirds of their courage and their skill at arms and their strength, and I will bind their urine in their own bodies and in the bodies of their horses.*

Finally, it remains to observe that though most references associate the *drui* and, very occasionally, the *faith* with the sacral function, a substantial number associate the *fili* with it as well. Like the *drui*, the *fili* has a pagan craft god: Brigit, daughter of the Dagda the god *of druidecht, was the goddess whom the filid* (plural of *fili*) *adored*[318]. Like the *drui*, the *fili* derives his wisdom from the Otherworld. The *fili* Néde mac Adnai describes the origin of the wisdom to which he lays claim in genealogical terms[319]:

> *I am the son of poetic art, son of meditation, son of thought, son of great vision, son of inquiry, son of investigation, son of great vision, son of great sense, son of understanding, son of knowledge, son of the three gods of poetic art.*

---

[314] Meyer 1907-13, 60
[315] O'Daly 1975, 50
[316] Fraser 1916, 42
[317] Gray 1982, 45
[318] Stokes 1862, 8
[319] Stokes 1905, 30

The *three gods of poetic art* are described as sons of Brigit daughter of the Dagda. As for the *druí*, there is a mythology whereby Otherworld knowledge comes to the *fili*: those who drink the *imbas* from the hazels *of* Segais become *primfilid* ('*filid* of the highest rank')[320]. There are graphic accounts of the rituals whereby *imbas* was attained by *filid*[321], and like the *druí* the *fili* thereby attains prophetic knowledge and magical powers[322] which he uses in the service of kings[323].

- The legal function

In what follows we shall be dealing with law tracts, which, as noted earlier, are in principle contemporary texts that relate to post-Conversion reality. These tracts do, however, often refer to their sources in a pre-Christian past which is the same as the one to which the King and Ulster Cycle tales refer. As reconstructions of the past by the post-Conversion learned elite, these references qualify as non-contemporary.

The introduction to *Senchas Már*, an extensive collection of law tracts, presents the general principles of the compilation and the sources of its authority[324]:

> *The senchas* ('tradition') *of the men of Ireland: what has preserved it? The joint memory of aged men, transmission from one ear to another, díchetal filed* ('the chanting of *filid'*), *addition from the law of the letter, strengthening from the law of nature. These are the strong rocks on which the bretha* ('legal judgments') *of the world are secured.*

In the view of the compiler(s) of the canonical stratum of *Senchas Már*, written law was at least in part based on oral tradition transmitted by *the chanting of filid.*

---

[320] Thurneysen 1927, 268; see further Breatnach 1981
[321] Stokes 1861, 25
[322] Meyer 1906, 22; Macalister 1938-56, vol5, 38, 56
[323] MacSweeney 1904, 103 ff; Stokes 1903, 192; Stokes 1900, 160
[324] Thurneysen 1926-7, 175; on *Senchas Mar* see Breatnach 1996

A slightly later[325] account makes this more explicit. It tells how St. Patrick revised pre-Christian Irish law to bring it into line with Christian scripture --the *law of the letter* of the passage just quoted[326]:

> (It is) natural law that was with the men of Ireland until the coming of the faith in the time of Lóegaire mac Néill. It is in his time that Patrick came. It is after the men of Ireland had believed in Patrick that the two laws were harmonised, natural law and the law of scripture. Dubthach maccu Lugair the poet (fili) displayed the law of nature...Dubthach maccu Lugair the poet recounted the judgments of the men of Ireland according to the law of nature and the law of the prophets. For prophecy according to natural law had prevailed in the judgment of the island of Ireland and in her poets (filid)...Dubthach, then, showed (this) to Patrick. That which did not contradict the word of God in the law of scripture and the consciences of Christians was harminised in the judicial order by the Church and the poets (filid).

Here again, the Christian compiler of this account saw custody of the law in pre-Christian times being in the hands of the *filid*.

Senchas Már and various other tracts cite legal pronouncements by pre-Conversion *filid*, which are regarded as definitive judgments handed down from time immemorial. Amargen, Athirne, and Ferchertne are all *filid* associated with the court of the Ulster king Conchobor at Emain Macha. *Heptads*, a constituent tract of *Senchas Már*, asks: *When was the customary law of suretyship established among the men of Ireland?*, and answers itself: *After Amargen fell liable, for it is he who first gave a surety after the infringement of law in Ireland*[327]. The tract *Córus Bretha Nemed* begins: *Concerning the judgments of the filid. Relate all, O*

---

[325] McCone 1986; Carey 1994
[326] McCone 1986, 21; see also McCone 1990 ch. 4
[327] Binchy 1978, 63, line 7

Amargen, speak the truth of the filid, the keen judgements of the excellent ones[328]; a paragraph in a tract dealing among other things with the honour price payable for various social grades is introduced: *O very praiseworthy Amargen, how shall I award the honour price of every person?*[329]; Athirne, described as *a sage of seven judgments,* is credited with a ruling on honour price[330]; and *the judgments of Ferchertne, of the truthful fili* are cited on the same subject[331].

We have already seen that *Senchas Már* regarded *'the chanting of the filid'* as the foundation of written law. Another tract, *Uraicecht Bec,* says that *the judgment of a fili is founded on roscada*[332]; *roscad* denotes a rhythmical alliterative form of verse not confined to legal subject matter but often associated with it[333], where it is typically introduced by the formula *as the traditional law sings it.* Such verse is quoted for authority, a further indication that the orally transmitted law of the *filid* was the primary form: the prose text of the tract makes a point and, to support it, quotes a short verse passage that says the same thing. Such *roscada* are often linked with pre-Conversion *filid* like Amargen, Athirne, and Néde mac Adnai[334].

The picture so far is complicated by the fact that another figure, the *brithem,* is associated alongside the *fili* with the cultivation of law. While the evidence for the relation of *brithem* to *fili* is important in the study of early Irish law generally, it is not directly relevant to the current discussion. In what follows, *fili* and *brithem* are used interchangably in relation to the legal function.

The *brithem* is often shown advising the king on legal matters brought before him. The tract *Gúbretha Caratniad,* for example, consists of a series of questions and answers in which Conn Cetchathach asks his *brithem* Caratnia about difficult points on a variety of legal matters. The introduction to it says: *Whatever*

---

[328] Binchy 1978, 2213, line 34
[329] Binchy 1978, 1125, line 1
[330] Binchy 1978, 1115, line 35
[331] Binchy 1978, 1113, line 14
[332] Binchy 1978, 1592, line 12
[333] MacCana 1966; Binchy 1972; McCone 1990 ch. 2
[334] Breatnach 1981, 63; also Binchy 1978, 1115, 1117, 1119, 1121

judgment was brought to Conn, Conn used to put it to Caratnia. And Conn used to ask him: 'What is the judgment you have given?[335]. A King Tale, *The Adventure of Cormac,* tells how two claimants to ownership of a sword appealed to King Cormac mac Airt about it, and how Cormac decided the case in consultation with his *brithem* Fithel[336]. *Conchobor [mac Nessa] and Sencha were appealed to for judgment* on how long an ordeal by battle can legally be delayed, and the *brithem* Sencha gives the decision[337]; in *The Conception of Cú Chulainn* Sencha describes himself as follows[338]:

> *I am an ollam, I am wise, I am not forgetful. I address every individual before the king. I prepare his speech. I judge in battle before battle-victorious Conchobor. I establish the legal judgments of the Ulstermen, and I do not stir them up.*

• The historical function

Members of the post-Conversion learned elite attributed preservation of historical tradition, and more particularly of royal dynastic tradition, in pre-Conversion times to the *fili*. This emerges from an analysis of that part of the main extant genealogical collections which deals with the Laigin, the royal dynasty of Leinster in the early medieval period[339].

The tract begins by stating its intention of integrating the Laigin's *names and their kings and their origins and their genealogies and divisions,* and proceeds to do so in three parts. Part I consists of four poems: a short one telling of the invasion and conquest of Leinster by one Labraid Loingsech, and three longer ones on the succession of allegedly early but actually legendary or mythical Laigin kings. Part II consists entirely of unadorned descent-lists for --in terms of the chronology of Part I-- very recently developed branches of the dynasty. Part

---

[335] 81 Thurneysen 1924-5, 306
[336] Stokes 1892, 199-202
[337] Binchy 1978, 406, line 26
[338] van Hamel 1933, 7
[339] O'Brien 1962, 1 ff and 334 ff; on this material see O Corrain 1985

III then starts over again with Labraid Loingsech, and goes on in systematic fashion to develop the descent of the Laigin from Labraid in a narrative that alternates verse and prose, where the verse is sometimes excerpted from the poems of Part I, until this narrative style gives way for more recent generations to descent lists like those of Part II. It is clear that Part II has been displaced by accident or design, and it is not referred to again.

The poems of Part I are older than the tract in which they occur. They have on linguistic grounds variously been dated to the seventh or sixth, and more recently even to the fifth century, but this is a technical matter, and it is dating relative to the rest of the tract, not absolute dating, that is important here[340]. The first step is to look at them independently of their context[341].

Poem 1 tells in highly compressed and allusive fashion how Labraid Loingsech brought the Laigin to Ireland from overseas, and how they took the name 'Laigin' from the spears they used to conquer Leinster. It is, in fact, the Laigin origin legend.

Poem 2 traces the genealogy of the mythical Laigin king Nuadu Necht through Labraid Loingsech as far back as Adam. It is not simply a list of names: each individual is praised to a greater or lesser degree in relation to specific events in his career. For example:

Nuadu Necht did not suffer bad rulership; Etarscél maccu Iair was killed, a ruler of great inheritance. A great leader of warriors against a fierce, constant king, red were the tributes of the swift grandson of Lugaid.

The third and fourth stanzas go on in similar fashion about Nuadu Necht's son:

A swift one in ships who crossed the sea as a warrior of the west, a red wind which coloured a bloody man on a sharp edge was Fergus

---

[340] Greene 1977; O Corrain 1985; Carney 1989
[341] For commentary see Meyer 1913, 1914

Fairrce, a strong descendant of Nuadu Necht, a great warrior who did not like to be dispossessed of his sovereignty.

The line of descent now proceeds backwards through Nuadu's ancestors. Labraid Loingsech's entry is noteworthy in that it consists not of the usual one or two stanzas, but of twelve, with considerable narrative detail which tells the same story as poem 1. Thereafter, poem 2 becomes a mere name-list until it gets to Adam, and the narrative element is dropped entirely.

Poem 3 is essentially a versified name-list with occasional descriptive or panegyric tags. It begins with one Énnae, and after a dozen or so names comes to Nuadu Necht, from where with minor variations it follows the same sequence as poem 2 to Labraid Loingsech. The remainder is a much inflated version of the biblical section of poem 2.

Poem 4 ennumerates successive Laigin kings of Tara starting with Labraid Loingsech, who is here as in the other poems described in heroic terms --*'a noble battle soldier fair and tall was Labraid Loingsech, a warlike lion, a helper celebrated in song, a powerful helper in battle*-- and continues with a series of names, similarly elaborated, which corresponds substantially to the non-biblical succession in poems 2 and 3.

Turning now to Part III, it is clear that the compiler of the tract here drew directly on the poems of Part I and on similar verse material in constructing a narrative early history of the Laigin dynasty, and that he regarded such verse as a definitive source of information on the subject. Part III begins by quoting a genealogy of Labraid Loingsech --*Labraid Loingsech son of Ailill Áine son of Loegaire Lorc son of Augaine Már, from whom the Laigin are descended*-- which is immediately followed by *as Laidcenn mac Bairchedo said,* and the relevant two lines from Poem 2; Laidcenn mac Bairchedo appears elsewhere as *fili* to Niall Noígiallach, the legendary founder of the Uí Néill dynasty[342]. Then comes some

---

[342] Stokes 1894, 295

prose telling how Labraid had come to Ireland from across the sea and destroyed Dind Ríg, an important fortress in Leinster; *as Ferchertne said* introduces a linguistically archaic poem[343] which tells how Dind Rig was destroyed and its defenders killed by *the fierce boar-champion Labraid, the warrior of Ireland, the grandson of Loegaire Lorc,* where Ferchertne is the *fili* who assumed the chair of *filidecht* ('the learning of the *fili*') in the Middle Irish *Colloquy of the Two Sages*[344]. *It is then that he took the kingship of Leinster, as Find mac Rossa says in the poem which he made,* the narrative goes on, describing in prose Labraid's accession to the kingship; Find mac Rossa, otherwise known as Find *fili*, is elsewhere in the tract credited with the composition of Poems 1 and 2. This is followed by a short verse extract on Labraid's marriage which is introduced by *as Ferchertne fili said. Labraid then took the kingship of the foreigners and went as far as the Alps, as Find fili said:* there follows a short quotation from Poem 2, after which Labraid's reign is rounded off with yet another quotation from linguistically archaic verse:

> *Lynx of a shield, white phantom, under the heavens there was no*
> *one who was a bright as the son of Áine. A man higher than gods,*
> *the solid seed of an oak, pure and well connected was the grandson*
> *of Loegaire Lorc.*

The tract now proceeds to an account of Labraid's successors. As before, it is mainly in prose but also includes some verse quotations of the sort already cited. One of these is attributed to Senchán Torpéist[345], who is said to have been the *fili* of Guaire, king of Connacht (died 663 AD). Another relates to a certain Art Mes Telmann and is credited to Briccéne mac Brígni, *a fili* of whom nothing further appears to be known:

> *A prince has gone into the land of the dead, the noble son of*
> *Sétnae. He ravaged the land of the Fomorians...From the top of the*

---

[343] Wagner 1977
[344] Stokes 1905
[345] Thurneysen 1931-3

142

fort of Ailenn he devastated the strong ones of the world, a great leader ruling over peoples, Mes Telmann of the Domnain.

The tract continues in this way, quoting further from poems by Find *fili* and Senchán Torpéist and from anonymous verse sources. It eventually gives way almost exclusively to descent-lists, with the notable exception of the account attached to Cathaír Már, where a full prose account is interspersed with numerous quotations from the poetry of the *fili* Lugair.

The compiler of the Laigin tract, then, had available a corpus of tradition relating to the early history of the Laigin royal dynasty. It included an account of the dynasty's foundation and of the early stages of descent which determined its shape in historical times. This tradition was in the form of verse in which historical narrative, genealogical information, and panegyric were interwoven, and the compiler(s) of the tract attributed such verse to mainly legendary, pre-Conversion *filid*.

- The panegyric function

In the Ulster Cycle tale *The Wooing of Emer*, the hero Cú Chulainn describes his youthful training at the royal court *among druid and filid and wise men*, saying: *I sat on the knee of Amargen fili, so that I can now praise the king for every excellence that he has*[346]. This captures another of the *fili's* functions: the composition and recitation of praise poetry before royalty in their courts. The function itself is called *bairdne*, 'bardism', in the sources. An Old Irish praise poem ends: *At ale there are panegyrics...pleasant bairdne celebrate through pools of liquor the name of Áed*[347]; Fiacc, a pupil of *the fili* Dubthach maccu Lugair in the tenth-century *Tripartite Life of Patrick*, is said to have gone *into the land of Connacht with bairdne for the kings*[348].

---

[346] van Hamel 1933, 29-30
[347] Stokes 1901, vol.2, 295
[348] Mulchrone 1939, 115

The priestly-learned order in contemporary references

This section aims to corroborate as much of the preceding account as possible using contemporary references, with the intention of showing that a secular learned class having certain of the features attributed to the pre-Conversion priestly-learned order by non-contemporary references existed in the early post-Conversion centuries.

At this time, a figure corresponding to the *druí* of the non-contemporary texts is extant but under pressure from the Church, and soon disappears from the contemporary record. The major figures are now the *fili*, who has lost the sacral characteristics which the non-contemporary texts attribute to him and who is now primarily associated with dynastic history and panegyric, and the *brithem*, who is the legal specialist. The *fili* of this period belongs to a hereditary social class, and is accorded a legal status equivalent to that of the king of a *túath* or of a bishop[349]. Of the *fili's* place within the *túath* in post-Conversion times, the law tract *Bretha Nemed* says[350]: A *túath without an ecclesiastical scholar, a church, a fili, and a king who makes contracts and external treaties between the túatha is no túath;* another tract, *Críth Gablach,* puts the *éces* --a synonym for *fili*--on the king's right hand, and the *brithem* on the left[351]. And, finally, the *fili* is paid for his services by his royal patron. *Bretha Nemed* says: *No fili is entitled to the due which corresponds to him* [ie, his legal status]...*until his strictly composed verses come forth*[352], and a legal poem in one of the metrical tracts sets out in detail the level of payment for various types of composition, quoting the legendary *fili* Amargen for authority[353].

---

[349] Breatnach 1987, 1988
[350] Binchy 1978, 1123, line 32
[351] Binchy 1941, 23
[352] Breatnach 1988, 38
[353] Thurneysen 1891, 31

- The sacral function

The *druí* is comparatively rarely mentioned in contemporary sources[354]. The references which do exist, however, are sufficient to show that a pagan priesthood had actually existed in pre-Conversion Ireland, and was not merely a literary artefact of the noncontemporary documentation invented by the post-Conversion learned elite for its own reasons. One of these is in the law tract *Uraicecht Bec* which, having ennumerated the *sáernemed*, 'higher nobility', proceeds to the *dáernemed*, strictly 'non-free nobility' but more accurately translatable as 'artisan class': *The dáernemed: carpenters and smiths and coppersmiths and craftsmen and leeches and judges and druíd and every other group besides*[355]. Another tract, *Bretha Crólige*, prescribes payment for injury due the various social classes:[356]

> *There are three persons among the people who are maintained according to the standard of maintenance of a freeman commoner...druí, reiver, satirist. For it is more fitting in the sight of God to repudiate them than to protect them.*

The early Irish legal tracts define a hierarchical social system in which status is crucial, and they are all directly or indirectly concerned with it because it determined the whole range of an individual's rights. Here the *druí is* accorded commoner status, but significantly he is not assigned to the unfree grades below the level of freeman commoner, an indication that he was still sufficiently well established at the time when the two tracts were compiled to rule out complete dismissal; that he was felt to be unacceptable *in the sight of God* by the Christian compiler of the tract is consistent with the *druí* portrayed in the non-contemporary texts.

Various ecclesiastical Latin texts indicate that a figure very like the *druí* continued to be prominent enough in the early post-Conversion centuries to annoy

---

[354] On what follows see also McCone 1990, 220 ff
[355] Binchy 1978, 1612, line 4
[356] Binchy 1938, sect. 51

the Church. The most important of these texts is, surprisingly, the Anglo-Saxon *Life of St. Guthlac* written c.740 AD and referred to earlier in the discussion of Anglo-Saxon historical tradition. It tells of a certain Bishop Headda who was on his way to see Guthlac, a hermit living in East Anglia and renowned for his magical powers. Some of the men in Headda's retinue *began to marvel at the miracles and wonders of the great man Guthlac*. One of them, Wigfrith, claimed to be able to tell whether the saint was *a follower of the true religion or merely a pretender to saintliness*; he goes on[357]:

> He said that he had lived among the Irish and there saw pseudo-
> anchorites following a variety of religions who claimed to be able
> to predict the future and perform magical feats by some numinous
> power which he did not understand. He also saw followers of the
> true religion performing signs and miracles...

on the basis of which experience he would be able to judge Guthlac. *Followers of the true religion performing signs and miracles* were familiar enough to an Englishman accustomed to hearing about Christian saints at home, but Wigfrith felt it necessary to distinguish between Christian holy men and *pseudo-anchorites,* whose resemblance to the *drui* of the non-contemporary texts is manifest. Because they were outsiders to contemporary Irish culture, the testimony of Wigfrith and Felix, the author of the *Life,* counts as objective observation and is consequently authoritative for Ireland at the time in question. The internal chronology of the *Life* indicates the later seventh century, about the time when, Bede says, numerous Anglo-Saxons went to Ireland to study. This objectivity introduces a difficulty, however. Neither Wiglaf nor Felix had an Irish writer's cultural awareness for interpreting or the terminology for describing what was observed, and they consequently described it in terms familiar to them: the *pseudo-anchorites* were like Christian holy men, but were not Christians. One might therefore object that the *Life* was perhaps referring to sects deviant from

---

[357] Colgrave 1956, 142-4

but still within the Christian tradition rather than to *druid*, but in such a case one would expect them to be described as *heretici* or *schismatici* rather than as belonging to *a variety of religions.*

There are also relevant references scattered among various early Hiberno-Latin texts. The late-sixth or early-seventh century *First Synod of Patrick*, for example, prescribes a penance for anyone who *in the manner of pagans swears an oath to a soothsayer*[358], and the (probably) seventh-century *Canones Hiberneses* class the *magus* among heretics, adulterers and malefactors who are deserving of particularly harsh punishment[359]; *magus* is the term used by roughly contemporary writers like to translate *druí*[360]. The eighth-century *Collectio Canonum Hibernensis* includes a long chapter entitled *De Auguriis*[361]. The tone is hostile, as one might expect. A sampling of section headings gives a good idea of the drift: *That Christians should not consult divinations or auguries; Concerning the penalties for Christians who observe divinations; Why demons know more than men.* And, finally, both the *Collectio* and the approximately contemporary *De Duodecim Abusivis Saeculi* contain a series of prescriptions to be observed by the ideal Christian king. One of them is that the king *ought to have old, wise, and sober counsellors, and not listen to the superstitions of magi or prophets or augurors*[362]. The authoritativeness of these references is based on the same argument as the one made for comparable Anglo-Saxon ecclesiastical texts earlier: that the Church is here condemning perceived abuses serious enough to warrant mention, not setting up straw men to knock down.

The *Life of St. Guthlac* and the Hiberno-Latin texts, then, tell us that a variety of holy men who were deeply offensive to Christianity, who claimed prophetic and magical powers, and who were consulted by kings existed in seventh and eighth-century Ireland. *Uraicecht Bec* and *Bretha Crólige* confirm the

---

[358] Bieler 1963, 56; Binchy 1968; Hughes 1972, 69 ff
[359] Bieler 1963, 160
[360] Bieler 1979
[361] Wasserschleben 1885, LXIV; Kenney 1929, 247-50; Hughes 1972, ch. 3
[362] Hellmann 1910, XII 51-2; Wasserchleben 1885, ch. xxv

existence of *druid* in Ireland at about this time. The essential features of the *drui* in the non-contemporary texts are thereby corroborated for early post-Conversion Ireland; because a pagan priesthood is not likely to have come into being precisely during the Conversion period, its seems reasonable to project that priesthood some indeterminate distance into the pre-Conversion past, as the non-contemporary texts do.

- The legal function

A Middle Irish legal commentary distinguishes two sorts of *brithem*[363]:

> There is a brithem proper to the people of the túath and a brithem proper to the king of a túath. Anything which the people of the túath prosecute among themselves, each of them against his fellow, and which is prosecuted against them from outside, it is their brithem who gives judgment concerning it. The brithem of the king of the túath: anything which the king of the túath prosecutes against the people of the túath, and which the people of the túath prosecute against him, and which is prosecuted against him from outside, his brithem it is who makes the judgment.

An 'historical' precedent for this distinction is attributed to the legendary king of Tara Cormac mac Airt in a conversation he is said to have had with his doorkeeper Bríathrach[364]. The latter asks: *O grandson of Conn, who is the brithem who should be appealed to concerning the legal relationship of neighbors in a territory?*. Cormac answers with a negative: *The high brithem who speaks true judgments in front of the king and the túath: it is not he who is to be consulted concerning the neighborhood law of a territory.* The *brithem* 'whom the king appoints...to deal with cases of what we now call public law'[365], can readily be shown to have existed in the post-Conversion period. In the tract *Críth*

---

[363] Binchy 1978, 1965, line 17
[364] Meyer 1918, 362-3; also O'Daly 1975, 74; Thurneysen 1924-5, 306; Stokes 1891, 199-202
[365] Binchy 1941, 79

Gablach the position of *brithem* is one of the *duties of a king to the túath that exalts him...They are entitled that he give them a just brithem*[366]. In the same tract the *brithem* appears in the royal hall sitting in a place of honour next to the king[367]; so important was he that, in the busy sowing season when the king's retinue was reduced to an absolute minimum he kept two attendants and his *brithem*[368]. And the *Annals of Ulster* record for 805 AD the death of *'Conmach iudex nepotum Briuin'*, where *iudex* is a direct translation of *brithem,* and the Uí Briúin the dominant branch of the royal dynasty of Connacht.

In the non-contemporary sources custody of the law was in the hands of the *fili* as well as of the *brithem,* but in contemporary texts it is rare for the *fili* to be associated with the law. The standard view is that a tendency towards specialisation in learning and function began to manifest itself in the wake of Christian conversion, whereby 'the *brithem* or expert in law gradually acquired an independent status', and 'instead of being subsumed under the designation of *filid,* the legal experts came more and more to be regarded as an autonomous class or profession'[369]. Certainly, by the time the law tracts were being redacted, the *fili* and the *brithem* were separate figures. *Crith Gablach* puts this graphically by seating the *brithem* on one side of the king, and the *éces* or *fili* on the other, as already noted[370]. The demarcation between the two figures is not quite this straightforward[371], but suffices for present purposes.

- The historical function

The custody of dynastic historical tradition which the Laigin tract attributes to pre-Conversion *filid* can be demonstrated for the early post-Conversion period; in fact, it can be shown to have persisted into the later

---

[366] Binchy 1941, 19-20
[367] Binchy 1941, 23
[368] Binchy 1941, 21
[369] MacCana 1970, 68
[370] Binchy 1941, 23
[371] MacCana 1970, McCone 1990

Middle Ages[372], but that is unnecessary for present purposes. One of the Middle Irish metrical tracts prescribes for the eighth year of training in *filidecht dindsenchas and primscéla of Ireland for reciting to kings and rulers and nobles*[373]. *Dindsenchas* translates literally as 'tradition of high places', and refers to the accumulation of myth and legend attaching to prominent topographical sites throughout Ireland. One of the Old Irish tales of the Mongán mac Fiachnai group[374] of King tales describes King Fiachnae mac Báetáin on a royal circuit with his *fili* Eochu, the *high fili of Ireland.* Coming to a series of standing stones, the king asks Eochu the history behind them; Eochu replies by drawing on his knowledge of Ulster Cycle tradition[375]. A large corpus of *dindsenchas* material survives[376], and a main collection is attributed in a Middle Irish prologue to Amargen mac Amalgado, a probably-historical *fili* of the seventh century[377]. Another long *dindsenchas* poem is reliably attributed to the *fili* Cináed ua hArtacáin, who died in 975 AD[378]. The reciting of *primscéla*, 'chief stories', before *kings and rulers and nobles* is exemplified, again in the Mongán mac Fiachnai tales, by Forgoll *fili* who, at Mongán's court, *recited a scél* ('story') *to Mongán every evening. So great was his knowledge that they were thus from autumn to spring*[379]. Similarly, the *fili* Urard mac Coise, who died in 980 AD, went to Domnall mac Muirchertaig, king of Tara[380]:

> The king asked for scéla from him after he had settled in. Urard
> told him that he had heard great scéla, for he could remember the
> coimgneda (see below) and scéla and senchusa ('histories') and
> gabála ('invasions') of Ireland according to what had happened

---

[372] Carney 1967, 1973; P. Breatnach 1983; Knott 1922-6, vol. 1, 218 and vol. 2, 144-5
[373] Thurneysen 1891, 50
[374] MacCana 1972b
[375] Knott 1916, 156
[376] Gwynn 1903-35
[377] Stokes 1894, 277
[378] Murphy 1952, 151 ff
[379] Meyer 1895, vol. 1, 45-6
[380] Byrne 1907-13, 42-3; Mac Cana 1980

from the frst conquest of Ireland after the Flood to the present time.

Urard then undertook to list for Domnall *the names of the coimgneda and the primscéla of Ireland;* there follows a list of titles which includes the extant King, Ulster, and Mythological Cycle tales. *Gabála* in the above-quoted passage refers to the body of tradition developed in the course of the early medieval centuries which synthesised native historical traditions with the bible and with world history taken from Orosius and Isidore of Seville[381]. *Senchas* (singular of *senchusa*) means 'history' or 'tradition' in general[382]. In the Middle Irish period, in other words, the *filid* were regarded as the custodians of broadly historical tradition, and were required to present this tradition when asked to by their royal patrons; the colophon to another such list of titles says simply: *He is no fili who does not preserve coimgne and all the scéla*[383].

Part of the *fili's* repertoire of historical tradition was dynastic history. The key term in showing this is *coimgne*[384], which has occurred several times in the foregoing discussion but has not thus far been translated. The *ollam*, the highest grade of *fili*, was legally required to be *knowledgable in every coimgne*[385]. The quotations in the preceding paragraph associate *coimgne* with terms referring to historical tradition in general, but it is closely linked with dynastic history in particular. *Bretha Nemed* says that the judgments of the legendary *fili* Ferchertne were characterised by *coimgne with poems...together with historical genealogies*[386]; this passage is excerpted in some commentary on *Uraicecht Bec*, which says: *the genealogies of the men of Ireland from Adam and their branches of blood relationship*[387]. Elsewhere in *Bretha Nemed* an obscure passage yields enough sense to show that *filid* compose *poems on coimgne*, to which the

---

[381] Byrne 1973, 9; O Corrain 1985; McCone 1990, ch. 3
[382] McCone 1990, ch. 3
[383] Best and O'Brien 1954-75, 837
[384] MacAirt 1958
[385] Breatnach 1987, sect. 2
[386] Binchy 1978, 1113, line 14
[387] Binchy 1978, 1603, line 39

commentator responds: *scéla or praise poems or songs and roscada, that is, senchas, that is, he has an abundance of synchronisms, he has the branches of blood relationship of every person as far as Adam*[388]. And, again in *Bretha Nemed*, a *fili* is required to provide *proper entertainment before every multitude in a festive drinking house, good speech on coimgne with the proper arrangement of blood relationship*[389]. The canonical stratum of *Bretha Nemed* therefore sees the seventh-eighth century *fili* as the custodian of historical-genealogical verse which he is required to recite to royal or aristocratic courts on public occasions. We have seen examples of just such verse attributed to pre-Conversion *filid* in the Laigin genealogical tract.

• The panegyric function

Panegyrics composed by *filid* of the early post-Conversion centuries for contemporary patrons are still extant. We shall look at some examples, and at the same time show how panegyric and dynastic history interacted.

The discussion of the poems in the Laigin genealogical tract drew attention to panegyrical elements in them, and these are manifest in the quoted excerpts. Conversely, panegyric often has an historical element. True, there is what one might call 'pure' panegyric, that is, verse having only laudatory content, such as the fragment of the poem which the *fili* Rechtgal úa Siadail composed on Donnchad mac Domnaill, king of Tara from 769 to 797 AD[390]:

> *Warlike king of the whole province of Ireland, high vehement one,*
> *mighty tree. He throws down --there is no peace-- every king except*
> *for the king of heaven.*

Such 'pure' panegyric may be an artefact of the circumstances of the poems' survival, however. Many of them are brief quotations in the metrical tracts where they are cited to exemplify some aspect of poetic style, and the nature of the full

---

[388] Binchy 1978, 1138, line 21
[389] Binchy 1978, 2219, line 20; Breatnach 1987, 37
[390] Meyer 1919, nr 7

poems from which they were excerpted is unknown. Most surviving panegyric verse praises its subjects in relation to specific events. One of them, for example, refers to events recorded in the *Annals of Ulster* for 839 AD, when *'Feidilmid, king of Munster, ravaged Míde and Breg, and remained in Tara'*. The corresponding poem says[391]:

> *Feidlimid is the king for whom it was the work of a day to unthrone*
> *Connacht without battle and devastate Míde.*

Such reference has self-evident potential to generate dynastic tradition. Two poems attributed to Dallán mac More, court *fili* to Cerball mac Muirecáin king of Leinster (885-909 AD)[392], will be used to show how panegyric with specific event reference could be the medium for the continuous generation of royal dynastic history.

In the first of the poems[393], Dallán begins by praising Cerball's nobility of descent, generosity, justice, and above all martial prowess in typical panegyric fashion. He then announces his purpose: *Innumerable his triumphs, which will be heard until Doom; his battles and encounters, each man shall hear them from me.* There follows a long versified list of battles that Cerball fought against various kings --in effect, a military *curriculum vitae*; the poem is an example of panegyric verse in which a king is praised in relation to specific events of his career.

The second poem[394] was composed for Cerball's nephew and intended successor Finn, and sets out Finn's qualities and achievements in the context of Laigin dynastic history. It is presented as an address to Cerball's sword, and offers a history of that sword in the hands of the earlier kings of Leinster who were also Finn's ancestors, the aim being a metaphorical expression of the consistently warlike and hence glorious character of that particular branch of the Laigin

---

[391] Meyer 1919, nr. 1
[392] Byrne 1973, 163-4 and 289
[393] Meyer 1908
[394] Meyer 1899

dynasty. It begins: *Hail, sword of Cerball, often have you been in the great woof of war...beheading high princes,* and proceeds to ennumerate those who had used it: *Forty years without sorrow Énnae of the noble hosts had you...Énnae gave you...to his own son Dúnlang.* In the genealogies Énnae is Énnae Nia, third in descent from Cathaír Már, who was in turn the progenitor of all important branches of the Laigin dynasty, and Dúnlang was the ancestor of one of the two most important of these, the Uí Dúnlainge, to which Cerball belonged. The poem then skips about a dozen generations with only a brief reference and moves on to Cerball's ancestors:

> *Thirty years you were in his possession: to Dúnlang you brought ruin. Many a king upon a high steed possessed you until Diarmait the kingly, the fierce; sixteen years was the time Diarmait had you. At the feast of Ailenn, a great time, Diarmait the hardy-born bestowed you, Diarmait the noble king gave you to the man of Mairge, to Muirecán. Forty years, with strength, you were in the hand of the high king of Ailenn. You were never a year without a battle while with Muirecán of the high deeds. In Tech Carmain Muirecán, overlord of the Vikings, gave you to; while he was in the world Cerball gave you to no one.*

At this point there are several quatrains in praise of the use to which Cerball put the sword in specific battles, three of which can be identified as historical events in the Annals. This second poem is in fact a history of the Uí Dúnlainge. It is also a panegyric, however. As the concluding lines show, the glory of the earlier Uí Dúnlainge kings was intended to redound on the man to whom the poem was actually addressed: *Who shall henceforth possess you?...You will not be neglected until you come to Tech Náis with strong fight, where Finn of the feasts is, they will say to you hail.*

Note what has happened to Cerball mac Muirecáin. The first of Dallán's poems praised him in relation to his exploits in war. In the second, Cerball and his exploits have been incorporated into family history.

Discussion

It has been argued that:

- An organised, high-status priestly-learned order existed in pre-Christian Ireland.

- This priestly-learned order served Irish lords by means of its sacral functions and its learning.

- A major aspect of the learning by which the order served lords was maintenance of and public recitation of dynastic history together with generation of new tradition via panegyric verse.

- The order survived the Christian Conversion and, suitably modified, continued to cultivate its learning in relation to lordship throughout the early medieval centuries.

These observations will not surprise specialists in Celtic Studies, but that is not the intention. Rather, the aim is to pull together evidence from a range of specialist studies and from texts which are typically little known outside the Celtic Studies field, and to focus it systematically on the topic of this book in a way that is generally accessible.

iii. Lordship and historical tradition among the Irish

As in Gaul and Anglo-Saxon England, the essence of panegyric was propaganda. It increased a leader's prestige by the public proclamation of his qualities in war and peace. The effects of the obverse, formal satire[395], show this very effectively: as praise builds up, so does satire destroy reputation and thus a ruler's authority. The Middle Irish commentary on *The Eulogy of Colum Cille*

---

[395] On satire see Robinson 1912; Meroney 1950-58; Ward 1973

says: *For, if he who was satirised did not perish at once, poisonous ulcers would grow on his face so that he was recognisable to everyone*[396]. In *Cormac's Glossary* the standard passage on the subject describes the *fili* Néde mac Adnai making a *glám díchinn*, a satire, on a king, *and three blisters came forth on his cheeks...He found on his face three blisters which the satire had caused, namely stain and blemish and defect. . . The king fled from there so that none would see his disgrace*[397]. And, in one of the Mongán mac Fiachnai tales, the *fili* Forgoll threatens a king who has offended him that *he would satirise him with his reproach, and he would satirise his father and his mother and his grandfather, and he would sing upon the waters so that fish would not be caught in the estuaries. He would sing upon their woods so that they would not give fruit, upon their plains so that they would be forever barren of any produce*[398]. In Irish law, status and honour are expressed in terms of *enech,* 'face', and the loss of these by 'reddening' or defiling of the face[399]. The blisters raised by the *fili's* satire are symbolic expressions of the loss of honour thereby occasioned, and the barrenness of the land as loss of authority, loss of honour meant losing all legal rights in the Irish social hierarchy.

From what has already been said, it is clear that the Irish court poet's panegyric verse could and did have an element of historical and more particularly dynastic historical tradition. As such, one can conclude that dynastic historical tradition was regarded by early Irish lords as a criterion for status, and that they had court poets to maintain and publicize such tradition.

The available evidence allows one to go further than this, however, and to show that dynastic history served to legitimise the prerogatives which Irish kings and their families claimed. This is generally recognised by historians of early

---

[396] Stokes 1898, 421
[397] Stokes 1862, xxxvi ff
[398] Meyer 1895, vol. 1, 46
[399] For example Binchy 1941, 12

Ireland[400]. In what follows, we shall be looking at one example: how the most successful of the early Irish dynasties, the Uí Néill, manipulated their own history for political ends.

The *fili*-verse described above was but one --albeit fundamental-- component in a complex of historical and genealogical tradition. Another was the *scéla*, and in particular the tales of the King Cycle. The King tales are as a genre not concerned with the history of Ireland in a broad sense, but with the histories of the main provincial dynasties of early medieval Ireland. The kings whose careers are documented are the same ones from whom the genealogical tracts draw the descent of these families: dynastic founders, their immediate descendants, progenitors of the main collateral branches. The fact that certain of the King tales actually occur in the tracts, where they serve to elaborate on early stages of descent, shows that the genealogists regarded them, like the *fili*-verse, as the historical foundation of their work. In fact, the tales themselves contain enough genealogical information to allow them to be arranged so as to yield more or less continuous narrative dynastic histories which correspond substantially to the schematisations of the tracts. One can, for example, elaborate on the descent which the tracts delineate for the Connachta and the Eóganachta --the ruling families of Connacht and Munster respectively-- with narratives that describe the careers and interrelationships of Conn Cétchathach, the eponymous founder of the Connachta, and Mug Nuadat, progenitor of the Eóganachta, along with the careers of their immediate descendants. To name only a few of the more obvious texts, *The Battle of Mag Léna, Concerning the reason for the wanderings of the Eóganachta, The Wooing of Momera,* and *The Vision of the Scál* are concerned with the times of Mug Nuadat and Conn; *The Battle of Mag Mucrama, Stories of Eógan and Cormac, Stories of Mosaulum,* and *The Battle of Cenn Abrat* deal with the next generation, and so on.

---

[400] O Cuiv 1963; Kelleher 1963; O Corrain 1973; Byrne 1973, 1974; O Corrain 1985, 1986; McCone 1990, ch. 10

The reason for wanting to connect the King tales with the historical-genealogical tradition cultivated by the *filid* is that they clearly exemplify the political application of such tradition. As a specific example, we can observe how traditions relating to the kingship of Tara, symbolically the most important royal title in early medieval Ireland, were manipulated in line with the claims to political hegemony which the Uí Neill made in the seventh and later centuries[401].

The Raid of the Collas[402] begins by deriving the Uí Néill, the Connachta, and the Airgialla from a common ancestor, Conn Cétchathach, a legendary king of Tara. It then sets out to explain, on allegedly historical grounds, why the Airgialla had no legitimate claim on the Tara kingship despite their descent. The burden of another text, *The Adventure of the sons of Eochu Muigmedón*[403], is to show why, among the remaining descendants of Conn, only Niall and his line were entitled to the kingship of Tara. The political intent of both texts is transparent; we shall examine the second in some detail.

Having come as far as Eochu Muigmedón, the section of the genealogical tracts which deals with the descendants of Conn gives a short prose account of how a *druí* guided Eochu in determining which of his sons would succeed him as king of Tara[404]:

> *Eochu Muigmedón, king of Ireland, asked his druí which of his sons would be king after him. It was then that Sithchenn, the druí of Tara, said: 'It will not be known until the forge is set on fire over them'. And the forge was set on fire. Then Brian, the eldest, took the chariot with its harness. Fiachrae took the vessels of wine. Ailill took the weapons. Niall took the tools of the smith: bellows, hammer, tongs, and the anvil with its block. 'It is true', said the*

---

[401] On the material which follows see O Corrain 1986
[402] O'Brien 1939
[403] Stokes 1903
[404] O'Brien 1962, 131

158

druí. 'Niall for supremacy, Fiachrae to reward you, Brian for your
judgments, Ailill for your warriors, Fergus to avenge you '.

There follows the *Testament of Niall*, a short document in which Niall disposes of
his inheritance to his sons, which is in turn followed by the observation that Niall
and Fergus were sons of one of the wives of Eochu Muigmedón, while Brian,
Fiachrae, and Ailill were sons by another wife, Mongfind. The potential for
political application should already be obvious; what this application is, and what
the *druí's* turgid interpretation might mean, emerges from the King tale *The
Adventure of the sons of Eochu Muigmedón.*

In that tale, the above forge motif and particulars of Niall's descent are part
of a narrative whose aim is to demonstrate on 'historical' grounds that the Uí Néill,
in spite of their common descent with the Connachta from Eochu Muigmedón,
had exclusive rights to the Tara kingship. It tells how Mongfind forced Eochu's
other wife, Niall's mother, to serve as a menial in Tara, and that Niall only escaped
being put to death by being spirited away soon after his birth by the *fili* Torna,
who fostered him until he was old enough to claim the kingship; on the occasion
of the rescue Torna recites a poem foretelling Niall's accession and naming him as
the progenitor of the line that was to control the Tara kingship forever. Now fully
grown, Niall arrives at Tara claiming succession rights, and Mongfind, worried
that her own sons might be shut out, demands that Eochu choose his successor
immediately. Eochu charges his *druí* with the decision: the forge episode follows,
and in it, as we have seen, Niall's pre-eminence is expressed in symbolic terms.
Mongfind is, however, dissatisfied with the verdict and requires Sithchenn --a
smith as well as a *druí*-- to forge weapons for all the brothers, who are then sent
hunting. Having stopped for the night, each of them sets out in turn to look for
water, and each meets an ugly hag who demands a kiss before she will allow water
to be taken from the well which she is guarding. Four of the brothers refuse, but
Niall, who meets her last of all, not only obliges but has sexual intercourse with

her. At this, she turns into a beautiful woman, identifies herself as Sovereignty[405], and proclaims: *The kingship and dominion will be forever with you and your descendants.* She then gives Niall water to drink and admonishes him: *Do not give water to your brothers until they make concessions to you: seniority over them, and that you may raise your weapon a hand's breadth over their weapons.* This Niall does --*he also bound them by oath never to oppose himself or his descendants*-- and they all return to Tara. On their arrival they all raise their weapons into the air, and Niall raises his higher than the others. Questioned about their adventures, the sons of Mongfind declare: *We gave our seniority and our kingship to Niall in return for water; You have given it permanently,* says the *drui, For henceforth he and his descendants will always have the dominion and the kingship of Ireland.*

This account is intelligible in the context of the Uí Néill position in early eleventh century Irish dynastic politics[406]. Tara had from earliest times been of special importance to the Laigin. Indications are they they struggled with the Uí Néill for control of it throughout the fifth and sixth centuries, until, by the final years of the seventh, it was firmly in Uí Néill hands. By that time, the Uí Néill were claiming political overlordship of the whole of Ireland for the king of Tara. The claim was not entirely convincing at first, but with the growth of Uí Néill power in subsequent centuries it came increasingly to approximate reality. *The Adventure of the sons of Eochu Muigmedón* is a transparent allegory of dynastic politics designed to show why the Uí Néill should have rights to Tara exclusive of the theoretically valid claim of their kinsmen, the Connachta. Niall is, first of all, differentiated along with Fergus, the progenitor of the politically inert and therefore non-threatening Uí Fergusa, from his brothers Brian, Fiachrae, and Ailill, the progenitors of the three main branches of the royal dynasty of Connacht, by descent from different mothers. This both admits kinship and weakens the

---

[405] MacCana 1955-6
[406] For what follows see MacNiocaill 1972, 9ff, 70 ff, 107 ff; Byrne 1973, chs. 4 and 5; O Corrain 1986, 145; McCone 1990, ch.10

160

genealogical bond. The indications from the forge episode that Niall was intended to succeed Eochu are confirmed by the second text, where both Fergus and the sons of Mongfind failed to grasp sovereignty when it was offered them, and Niall immediately did so. The others, moreover, resigned their claim to 'seniority' and their right to the Tara kingship for a share in the royal draught bestowed by Sovereignty; part of the argument here is that the kingship of Connacht, which belonged to the Uí Briain, the Uí Fiachrach, and the Uí Ailello, came to them via Niall. Other points of political symbolism such as Niall's right to raise his sword higher than his brothers', and the oath *never to oppose himself or his descendants*, further show that the purpose of tale *The Adventure of the sons of Eochu Muigmedón* was not entertainment or accurate recording of history, but justification of contemporary politics on pseudo-historical grounds.

4. CONCLUSION

The aim of this study has been to develop one aspect of Wenskus' theory that the evolution and maintenance of tribal traditions were essential to the ethnic identity and thus the long-term existence of barbarian European population groups, and that such traditions were typically propagated by the politically dominant stratum within such groups: the role of orally transmitted historical tradition in the legitimisation of lordship. That aim was to be realised as an hypothesis about the interaction of lordship and orally transmitted historical tradition among a range of barbarian European population groups, and the empirical support for that hypothesis was to be constructed using a two-stage methodology. Stage 1 was to involve identification of the groups for which a useful amount of relevant documentary evidence was available, and study of the evidence for each group using source criticism to arrive at a maximally plausible reconstruction in each case. Stage 2 would then use corroborative method to establish those features of the relation between lordship and historical tradition which were most likely to be true of barbarian European peoples in general. The foregoing discussion constituted Stage 1. This concluding section is Stage 2.

Corroborative method in the present application requires that the evidence for each of the groups included in the study be shown to be independent. Unfortunately, there is no prospect of being able to do this. It is in general possible to show that writer x **did** use writer y's work by demonstrating textual borrowing or influence, or arguing on various grounds that he is likely to have done so. Apart from the obvious special case of a given writer being unable to use work which postdates his, however, it cannot be shown that writer x **did not** use writer $y's$ work: absence of formal textual criteria or of strong plausibility arguments for borrowing does not logically imply that there was no borrowing. That being so, the application of corroborative method in the present case depends on a weaker condition than demonstrable independence: the unlikelihood of any large-scale interdependence of the sources used in this study. Specifically:

1. This study has referred to a large number of texts spread over broad geographical and chronological spans. Given the conditions which prevailed in late Antiquity and the early medieval centuries, it seems unlikely that most of our writers had most of the relevant earlier and contemporary material available for their use.

2. Even assuming that most of our writers had most of the earlier and contemporary materials available, what motivation would there be for them to use it for their own purposes? Why would Alcuin refer to Tacitus when fulminating against secular poets at Lindisfarne, for example, or the compilers of the Irish genealogies to Posidonius when attributing the origin of their materials to the oral traditions of the *filid*?

There is no obvious way to quantify the degree of unlikelihood involved here. Opinions about it will differ, and with them the conviction which the following reconstruction carries.

The Introduction stated the hypothesis. The approach here will be to work through it, summarizing for each of its claims the empirical support which it receives from the individual case studies.

- *At least some European barbarian population groups maintained orally transmitted traditions which included origin legends and accounts of notable leaders and events in their histories, often in the form of song.*

The groups included in the study were chosen because there is evidence that they maintained such historical traditions. In all cases, the traditions contained accounts of rulers and heroes of the past. With one possible exception, they featured origin legends: the Mannus genealogy for the early Germans; the departure from Scandinavia together with the account of the *ansis* at the head of the Amal genealogy for the Goths; the departure from Scandinavia and the Woden episode for the Lombards; the early Frankish wanderings leading to Merowech; the Kentish invasion story for the Anglo-Saxons; the Laigin origin account. The only doubtful case is that of the Gauls, where the story of the Celtic migration out of Gaul during the reign of King Ambigatus is not certainly Gaulish in origin. In all cases there is some reference to the traditions being formalised in song.

- *These traditions could include histories of specific ruling dynasties*

In several cases the traditions included dynastic historical elements: the Gothic Amal genealogy; the Frankish Merovingian-Carolingian dynastic material; the Kentish, Mercian, and very probably East Anglian dynastic histories together with similar histories which probably underlie the genealogical lists of the other major Anglo-Saxon ruling families; the Irish Laigin dynastic history. For the Gauls there is just enough evidence --the Gaulish aristocrats breaking forth into *'a song in praise of the valiant deeds of their ancestors'*-- to indicate the existence of family tradition. Among the Lombards there is no direct evidence for dynastic history, and for Tacitus' early Germans the only explicitly genealogical tradition is the origin legend tracing the descent of what appear to be population groups rather than dynasties from a god.

- *Barbarian lords legitimised their authority by associating themselves with such historical traditions, and by manipulating them so as to justify the current political status quo on historical grounds.*

Among the Anglo-Saxons, the Gauls, and the Irish, the court poet's panegyric verse legitimised the lord's authority by publicizing his qualifications to rule, and one of these qualifications was association with historical and more specifically dynastic tradition. The *scop* in *Beowulf* celebrates Beowulf in relation to a great hero of the past; Bituitus' Gaulish bard praises him in terms of his family history; the interaction of panegyric and dynastic history is everywhere manifest in the relevant Irish evidence. The legitimacy gained from association with dynastic history is also attested independently of the *scop* and his panegyric for the Anglo-Saxons, as well as for the Goths and the Franks; Rothari did the same with Lombard tribal history, and it may be significant that he included some genealogical information about himself.

Ireland offers an explicit and detailed account of how dynastic history could be and was manipulated to legitimize the political status quo. Far less detailed but nevertheless closely comparable is the case of the Semnones, who used the tradition of descent from the tribal god to legitimize their dominant position among the Suebi. The Anglo-Saxon genealogies can, moreover, be interpreted as reflecting manipulation of dynastic traditions in line with current political circumstances.

Now, there a difficulty with respect to what has just been said. The central argument of this discussion is that barbarian European lords exploited their historical traditions to legitimize their authority. We have seen the evidence for the existence of historical tradition across a range of barbarian groups, and can reasonably assert that these groups really did cultivate such traditions. The problem arises because the evidence for their political application comes to us via literate interpreters: Greek and Roman authors in Antiquity, and Christian ecclesiastical writers in the early middle ages. Tacitus interprets the significance of the Semnones' ritual for us, and information about the Gauls comes from the likes of Caesar and Posidonius. Cassiodorus constructed the Gothic Amal genealogy. Rothari and Charlemagne had Lombard and Frankish traditons written down, necessarily by churchmen and perhaps on their advice. Ecclesiastical writers compiled the Anglo-Saxon genealogies and the West Saxon collection of royal documents. The Irish Uí Néill texts were produced in a monastic environment. What reason, therefore, is there to think that political exploitation of historical tradition was a barbarian phenomenon at all? Perhaps it is an artefact of the literate cultures of Antquity and the early middle ages. The argument in favour of a barbarian rather than a literate origin is twofold:

i. The evidence for the existence of court poets among the Anglo-Saxons, Gauls, and Irish is such that their existence and characteristics as developed in the individual case studies cannot reasonably be doubted; on this see below. These court poets were a feature of barbarian culture, and so, consequently, was their legitimisation of lordship by association with historical tradition. In these three groups, therefore, the political application of historical tradition was a demonstrably barbarian phenomenon.

ii. One of the fundamental results of anthropological research on the function of oral tradition in non-literate societies is that such tradition is not what might be regarded as an optional extra --a source of entertainment, perhaps, on a dark evening. Rather, it is what defines a society's ethnic consciousness, and both motivates and maintains its institutions; this was Wenskus' point. And, more specifically, historical and genealogical tradition in non-literate societies is typically subject to revision according to social or political need at any given time[407]. Why, in this light, would the European groups we have discussed maintain historical traditions, and in at least three and perhaps four cases have had high-status court poets attached to royal courts as custodians of these traditions, if the traditions were not useful to lords? In other words, from an anthropological point of view, the very existence of these traditions and of the court poets who cultivated them strongly indicates that the exploitation by lords which we have seen had its origin in barbarian European culture.

---

[407] Goody 1978; Vansina 1985

- *In some groups the maintenance of historical tradition and its application to the legitimisation of lordship was institutionalised in professional poets. These poets were attached to the courts of the lords whom they served, and enjoyed a high social status on account of the service which they offered. The essence of this service was to publicize the patron's qualifications for lordship, and it had two main aspects: (i) maintenance of historical tradition, and of his patron's dynastic history in particular, and (ii) public celebration of the patron in terms of his personal qualities and of his association with the relevant historical tradition. The court poet's celebratory verse generated new tradition which could be incorporated into the existing corpus, thereby ensuring continuity.*

Court poets are attested for the Gauls, the Irish, the Anglo-Saxons, and the Franks. We will deal with the Celtic and Germanic examples separately.

The Irish court poet on the one hand maintained his patron's dynastic traditions, and on the other composed panegyrics on his patron's behalf; both were in verse form and were recited on public occasions. The evidence for the Gaulish court poet is much less extensive, but his role as panegyricist emerges clearly, and it is just sufficient to show him as custodian of historical and more narrowly dynastic tradition. Both poets were, moreover, associated with a priestly-learned order which enjoyed a high social status and exercised considerable influence over kings.

There is a terminological correspondence between the Irish and Gaulish priestly-learned orders: the Irish *drui* corresponds to the *druides* of the Classical texts, the Irish *fáith* to the *vates*, and the *bard* to the *bardi*. Moreover, the functions attributed to these orders coincide comprehensively; the foregoing discussion covers some aspects of this coincidence, but a much more detailed account can be and is constructed by the associated research literature[408]. In principle one could argue that this is due to Irish borrowing

---

from Classical sources, but in practice it would be difficult to establish a convincing argument. Even assuming that the relevant texts were known in early Ireland, one would have to explain

i. why Irish writers should have seen the Classical accounts as relevant to their work: it is not clear that the Irish knew they were Celts.

ii. why the Irish writers should have elaborated so extensively on their supposed sources: the Irish accounts describe their priestly-learned order in much greater detail than the Classical ones.

iii. how these writers managed to innovate fundamental aspects of early Irish social order --the *fili*, *brithem*, and *bard* together with the *druí* which they found so antithetical-- on the basis of the supposed Classical sources: the existence and characteristics of these figures are attested in contemporary early medieval Irish documentation, and are beyond reasonable doubt.

The alternative is to accept that, though groups who happen to speak related languages but are widely separated in space and time do not necessarily share social institutions, in the present instance it is a matter of empirical fact that they did. In other words, one can accept that the Gaulish and Irish bodies of evidence are at least substantially independent, and can therefore be used corrboratively to establish the existence of a common Celtic priestly-learned order with a range of corresponding characteristics.

Turning to the Germanic examples, there is a good case for thinking that the Anglo-Saxon *scop* had the status of a royal retainer, and that he served his patron by reciting panegyric and historical tradition, and dynastic tradition

---

[408] Caerwyn Williams 1971; Le Roux 1986; Beresford Ellis 1994; Ross 1995; Birkhan 1997, 896 ff.

more particularly, on public occasions. The Frankish court poet was a panegyricist, but there is no explicit link with contemporary Frankish historical tradition, and nothing is known of his status in the court.

The relationship between panegyric and historical tradition could only be shown for Ireland and Anglo-Saxon England.

The evidence for the Celtic court poet and for the priestly-learned order with which he is associated is much more extensive and detailed than that for his Germanic equivalent. One could argue that this reflects a substantive difference --that the elaborate priestly-learned order of the Celts had no counterpart among the Germanic peoples. In fact, Caesar says precisely that[409]. On the other hand, the disparity might simply reflect chance survival of evidence; Caesar's view can be counterbalanced with a passage from Bede's *Ecclesiastical History*, where the advisors of King Edwin of Northumbria included a pagan priest and what might just be a court poet[410]. No useful conclusion seems possible.

- *The cultivation of orally-transmitted tradition and of its political exploitation by lords survived long into the period of early medieval Christian literacy in several cases.*

The early Germans, the Gauls, and the Goths are ruled out here on account of their date. Among the Lombards orally transmitted historical tradition was used by King Rothari in the mid-seventh century and was still available to Paul the Deacon at the end of the eighth. Charlemagne had access to Frankish traditions shortly after 800 AD, and these were still known to his son Louis the Pious in the early ninth century and to Poeta Saxo in the late ninth. Among the Anglo-Saxons, court poets were active at least until the end

---

[409] Seel 1961, VI.21
[410] Colgrave & Mynors 1969, II/13

of the eighth century, and in Ireland to the end of our period, that is, up to c.1000 AD.

Let us summarize. The various Germanic and Celtic groups included in this study represent a good chronological, geographical, and ethnic sample of barbarian European groups. Given the agreement across all cases, it can be said that the cultivation of historical and more particularly dynastic tradition, and the exploitation of it by lords for legitimisation of their authority, was a general characteristic. Whether the existence of court poets was equally general is less certain, since they are attested in only four out of seven cases. Their social status ranges from that of the Celtic poet, who was both in Gaul and Ireland associated with an influential, high-status priestly-learned order, though the Anglo-Saxon *scop*, who there is good reason to believe was a land-holding member of his patron's court, to the Frankish poet about whom we know nothing. The Gaulish, Irish, and Anglo-Saxon court poets cultivated both historical tradition and panegyric, but only the latter function is attested for the Frankish one. The role of panegyric as generator of historical tradition is made explicit in only two cases, the Irish and the Anglo-Saxon. And, finally, this quintessentially barbarian, non-literate institution managed to survive for centuries into the nominally literate Christian early middle ages among the Lombards, Franks, Anglo-Saxons, and Irish; this accords well with Richter's findings with regard to general oral culture in early medieval Europe[411].

---

[411] Richter 1994, ch. 11

5. BIBLIOGRAPHY

Aitchison, N. (1987) 'The Ulster Cycle: heroic image and historical reality', *Journal of Medieval History* 13, 87-124

-- (1994) *Armagh and the royal centres in early medieval Ireland*, Boydell & Brewer

Alexander, M. (1983) *Old English Literature*, Macmillan

Baesecke, G. (1941) *Vor- und Frühgeschichte des deutschen Schrifttums*, Max Niemeyer Verlag

Barnwell, P. (1997) *Kings, courtiers, and imperium. The barbarian West 565-725*, Duckworth

Barratt, P. (1979) M. *Annaei Lucani belli civilis liber V*, Hakkert

Bassett, S. (1989b) 'In search of the origins of Anglo-Saxon kingdoms', in *The Origins of Anglo-Saxon Kingdoms*, ed. S. Bassett, Leicester University Press

Bately, J. (1986) *The Anglo-Saxon Chronicle: Ms. A*, D.S.Brewer. Cambridge

Beresford Ellis, P. (1990), *The Celtic Empire*, Constable

-- (1994), *The Druids*, Constable

Bergin, O. (1927) How the Dagda got his magic staff, in *Medieval Studies in memory of G. Loomis*, Columbia University Press

-- (1970) *Irish Bardic Poetry*, ed. D. Greene and F. Kelly, Dublin Institute for Advanced Studies

Best, R. (1907) 'The adventures of Art son of Conn and the courtship of Delbchaem', *Eriu 3*, 149-73

Best, R. & O'Brien, M. (1954-75) *The Book of Leinster*, 6 vols. , Dublin Institute for Advanced Studies

Beumann, H. (1966) 'Die deutschen Stämme im Reiche Karls des Grossen', in *Karl der Grosse*, ed. W. Braunfels, 2nd ed., L. Schwann Verlag

Bieler, L. (1963) *The Irish Penitentials*, Dublin Institute for Advanced Studies

-- (1979) *The Patrician texts in the Book of Armagh*, Dublin Institute for Advanced Studies

Binchy, D. (1938) *'Bretha Crolige'*, *Eriu* 12, 1-77

-- (1941) *Crith Gablach*, Medieval and Modern Irish Series XI, Stationery Office

-- (1943) 'The linguistic and historical value of the Irish law tracts', *Proceedings of the British Academy* 29, 195-227

-- (1968) 'St. Patrick's First Synod', *Studia Hibernica* 8, 49-59

-- (1970) *Celtic and Anglo-Saxon Kingship*, Clarendon Press

-- (1972) 'The so-called 'rhetorics' of Irish saga', in *Indo-celtica. Gedächtnisschrift für Alf Sommerfelt*, ed. H. Pilch, Hueber Verlag

-- (1978) *Corpus Iuris Hibernici*, , Dublin Institute for Advanced Studies

Birch, D. (1989) *Language, literature, and critical practice*, Routledge

Birkhan, H. (1997) *Kelten. Versuch einer Gesammtdarstellung ihrer Kultur*, Verlag der österreichischen Akademie der Wissenschaften

Blackburn, S. (1994) *The Oxford Dictionary of Philosophy*, Oxford University Press

Bloomfield, M. & Dunn, C. (1989) *The role of the poet in early societies*, D.S. Brewer

Bluman, A. (1992) *Elementary Statistics*, W.C.Brown Publishers.

Braunfels, W. (1966) *Karl der Grosse*, 2nd ed, L. Schwann Verlag

Breatnach, L. (1981) *'The cauldron of poesy'*, *Eriu* 32, 45-93

-- (1984) 'Canon law and secular law in early Ireland: the significance of *Bretha Nemed'*, *Peritia* 3, 439-59

-- (1987) *Uraicecht na Riar. The poetic grades in early Irish law*, Dublin Institute for Advanced Studies.

-- (1988) 'The first third of *Bretha Nemed Toisech'*, *Eriu* 40, 1-40

-- (1996) 'On the original extent of the *Senchas Mar*', *Eriu* 47, 1-44

Breatnach, P. (1983) 'The chief's poet', *Proceedings of the Royal Irish Academy* 83, 37-79

Brennan, B. (1984) 'The image of the Frankish kings in the poetry of Venantius Fortunatus', *Journal of Medieval History* 10, 1 - 11

Brooks, N. (1989) The creation and early structure of the kingdom of Kent, in The Origins of Anglo-Saxon Kingdoms, ed. S. Bassett, Leicester UP

Brunholzl, F. (1975) *Geschichte der lateinischen Literatur des Mittelalters*, Fink Verlag

Byrne, F. (1973) *Irish kings and high kings*, Batsford

-- (1974) '*Senchas*. The nature of Gaelic historical tradition', *Historical Studies* 9, 137 - 59

Byrne, M. (1907-13) *Airec Menman Uraird mac Coisse, in Anecdota from Irish Manuscripts*, ed. O. Bergin et al, Max Niemeyer Verlag

Caerwyn Williams, J. (1971) 'The court poet in medieval Ireland', *Proceedings of the British Academy* 57, 85 - 135

-- (1979-80) 'Posidonius' Celtic parasites', *Studia Celtica* 14-15, 313-43

Caerwyn Williams, J. & Ford, P. (1992) *The Irish Literary Tradition*, University of Wales Press

Campbell, A. (1962) *The Chronicle of Aethelweard*, Nelson

Cann, R. (1993) *Formal semantics. An introduction*, Cambridge University Press

Carey, J. (1994) 'An edition of the pseudo-historical prologue to the *Senchas Mar*', *Eriu* 45, 1-32

Carney, J. (1940) 'Nia son of Lugna Fer Tri', *Eigse* 2, 187-97

-- (1967) *The Irish bardic poet*, Dolmen Press

-- (1973) 'Society and the bardic poet', *Studies* 62, 233-50

-- (1989) 'The dating of archaic Irish verse', *in Early Irish Literature. Media and Communication*, ed. S. Trauter & H. Tristram, Gunter Narr Verlag

Carr, P. (1990) *Linguistic realities*, Cambridge University Press

Chadwick, H.M. (1907) *The Origin of the English Nation*, Cambridge University Press

Chadwick, N.K. (1966) *The Druids*, University of Wales Press

Chambers, R. (1959) *Beowulf. An Introduction*, 3rd ed., Cambridge University Press

Chaney, W. (1970) *The cult of kingship in Anglo-Saxon England*, Manchester University Press

Charles-Edwards, T.M. (1980) 'Review article: the *Corpus Iuris Hibernici'*, *Studia Hibernica* 20, 141-62

-- (1988) 'Early medieval kingships in the British Isles', in *The Origins of Anglo-Saxon Kingdoms*, ed. S. Bassett, Leicester University Press

-- (1993) *Early Irish and Welsh kingship*, Oxford University Press

Chase, C. (1981) *The dating of Beowulf*, University of Toronto Press

Christie, N. (1995) *The Lombards*, Blackwell

Colgrave, B. (1956) *Felix's Life of St. Guthlac*, Oxford University Press

Colgrave, B. & Mynors, R. (1969*) Bede's Ecclesiastical History of the English People*, Oxford University Press

Comyn, D. & Dinneen, P. (1902-14) *The History of Ireland*, Irish Texts Society 4,8,9,15

Crosby, H. & Cohoon, J. *Dio Chrysostom*, Loeb Classical Library, Heinemann

Cunliffe, B. (1979) *The Celtic World*, Bodley Head

-- (1988) *Greeks, Romans, and Barbarians*, Batsford

Dauge, Y.A. (1981) *Le barbare. Recherches sur la conception romaine de la barbarie et de la civilisation*, Latomus

176

de Jackson, J. (1989) *Historical criticism and the meaning of texts*, Routledge

Dillon, M. (1952) 'The story of the finding of Cashel', *Eriu* 16, 61-73

-- (1958) *The Cycles of the Kings*, Oxford University Press

Dilts, M. (1974) *Claudius Aelianus. Varia Historia*, Teubner

Dobbs, M. (1922) 'La bataille de Leitir Ruibhe', *Revue Celtique* 39, 1-32

-- (1923) 'The battle of Findchorad', *Zeitschrift für celtische Philologie*, 14, 395-420

Drinkwater, J.F. (1983) *Roman Gaul. The three provinces 58 BC - AD 260*, Croom Helm

Dümmler, E. (1895) *Alcuini Epistolae*, Monumenta Germaniae Historica. Epistolae Karolini Aevi 2

Dumville, D. (1976) 'The Anglian collection of royal genealogies and regnal lists', *Anglo-Saxon England* 5, 23-50

-- (1977) 'Kingship, genealogies, and regnal lists', *in Early Medieval Kingship*, ed. P. Sawyer & I. Wood, published by the editors

-- (1981) 'Beowulf and the Celtic world: the uses of evidence', *Traditio* 37, 109-60

-- (1985a) 'The *Historia Brittonum*: the 'Vatican' recension', D.S.Brewer

-- (1985b) 'On editing and translating medieval Irish chronicles: the *Annals of Ulster*', *Cambridge Medieval Celtic Studies* 10, 67-86

-- (1989) 'Essex, Middle Anglia and the expansion of Mercia in the south-east Midlands', in *The Origins of Anglo-Saxon Kingdoms*, ed. S. Bassett, Leicester University Press

Eliason, N. (1966) 'Two Old English scop poems', *Proceedings of the Modern Language Association of America* 81, 185-92

Ellis-Evans, D. (1980-82) 'Celts and Germans', *Bulletin of the Board of Celtic Studies* 29, 230-55

Falconer, W. (1946) *Marcus Tullius Cicero. De divinatione*, Loeb Classical Library, Heinemann

Field, P. (1996) 'Nennius and his history', *Studia Celtica* 30, 159-65

Foley, J. (1988) *The theory of oral composition*, Indiana University Press

Ford, P. (1990) 'The blind, the dumb, and the ugly: aspects of poets and their craft in early Ireland and Wales', *Cambridge Medieval Celtic Studies* 19, 27-40

Foster, B. (1919) *Livy*, Loeb Classical Library, Heinemann

Fouracre, P. & Gerberding, R. (1996) *Late Merovingian France. History and hagiography 640-720*, Manchester University Press

Fraser, J. (1915) 'The first battle of Moytura', *Eriu* 8, 1-63

French, W. (1945) 'Widsith and the *scop*', *Proceedings of the Modern Language Association of America* 50, 623-30

Gaechter, P. (1970) *Die Gedächtniskultur in Irland*, Institut für vergleichende Sprachwissenschaft der Universität Innsbruck

George, J. (1992) *Venantius Fortunatus. A poet in Merovingian Gaul*, Clarendon Press

Gerberding, R. (1987*)* *The rise of the Carolingians and the Liber Historiae Francorum*, Clarendon Press

Girvan, R. (1971) *Beowulf and the Seventh Century*, Manchester University Press

Goffart, W. (1980) *Barbarians and Romans AD 418 - 584. The techniques of accommodation*, Princeton University Press

-- 1988) *Tha narrators of barbarian history (AD 550 - 800)*, Princeton University Press

Goody, J. (1978) 'Oral tradition and the reconstruction of the past in northern Ghana', Fonti Orali - Oral Sources - sources orales. Antropologia e Storia - Anthropology and History - Anthropologie et Histoire, ed. B. Bernardi, C. Poni, A. Triulzi, Milan, 285-95

Gordon, E. (1976) *The Battle of Maldon*, Manchester University Press

Gossman, L. (1990) *Between history and literature*, Harvard University Press

Grabowski, K. & Dumville, D. (1984) *Chronicles and annals of medieval Ireland and Wales*, Boydell Press

Graus, F. (1963) Review of Wenskus 1961, *Historica* 7, 185-91

-- (1965) *Volk, Herrscher, und Heilger im Reiche der Merowinger*, Nakladatelstvi Ceskoslovenske Akademie Ved

Gray, E. (1982) '*Cath Maige Tuired*. The Second Battle of Mag Tuired', *Irish Texts Society*

Green, M. (1995) *The Celtic World*, Routledge

-- (1977) 'Archaic Irish', in *Indogermanisch und Keltisch*, ed. K.H. Schmidt, Reichert Verlag

Gschwantler, O. (1976) 'Die Heldensage von Alboin und Rosimund', *in Festgabe für Otto Höfler*, ed. H. Birkhan, Verlag Notring

-- (1979) 'Formen langobardischer mündlicher Überlieferung', *Jahrbuch für internationale Gerrnanistik* 11, 58-85

Gulick, C. (1927) *The Deipnosophists*, Loeb Classical Library, Heinemann

Gwynn, E. (1903-35) *The metrical dindsenchas*, 5 vols., Royal Irish Academy

-- (1942) 'An Old Irish tract on the privileges and responsibilities of poets', *Eriu* 13, 1-60 and 220-36

Haddan, A. and Stubbs, W. (1871*) Councils and ecclesiastical documents relating to Great Britain and Ireland*, Oxford University Press

van Hamel, A. (1933) *Compert Con Culainn and other stories*, Medieval and Modern Irish Series III, , Dublin Institute for Advanced Studies

Hamilton, N. (1870) *Willelmi Malmesbiriensis monachi De Gestis Pontificum Anglorum*, Rolls Series

Hammond, N. & Scullard, H. (1970) *The Oxford Classical Dictionary*, 2nd ed., Clarendon Press

Harbison, P. (1988) *Pre-Christian Ireland*, Thames and Hudson

Haubrichs, W. (1988) 'Die Anfänge', *in Geschichte der deutschen Literatur von den Anfängen bis zum Beginn der Neuzeit*, ed. H. Heinzle, Athenäum Verlag, Band 1

Hauck, K. (1955) 'Lebensnormen und Kultmythen in gerrnanischen Stammes- und Herrschergenealogien', *Saeculum* 6, 186-223

-- (1964) 'Carmina antiqua', *Zeitschrift fur bayerische Landesgeschichte* 27, 1-33

Hellmann, S. (1910) 'Pseudo-Cyprianus. *De XII abusivis saeculi', Texte und Untersuchungen zur Geschichte der altchristlichen Literatur* 34, 1-62

Heusler, A. (1911) 'Dichtung', in *Reallexikon der germanischen Altertumskunde*, ed. J. Hoops, K.J. Trübner Verlag

-- (1923) *Die altgerrnanische Dichtung*, Akademische Verlagsgesellschaft Athenaion

-- (1941) *Die altgerrnanische Dichtung*, 2nd ed., Akademische Verlagsgesellschaft Athenaion

Higham, N. (1995) *An English empire. Bede and the early Anglo-Saxon kings*, Manchester University Press

Hirsch, P. & Lohmann, H. (1935*) Widukind von Corvei. Rerum gestarum Saxonicum libri tres*, Monumenta Germaniae Historica. Scriptores rerum Germanicarum in usum scholarum, 5th edition

Höfler, O. (1973), 'Abstamrnungstraditionen', *in Reallexikon der germanischen Altertumskunde*, 2nd ed., ed. H. Beck, Walter de Gruyter

Holder, A. (1896) *Altkeltischer Sprachschatz*, Teubner Verlag

Holthausen, (1963) F. *Altenglisches etymologisches Wörterbuch*, 2nd ed., Winter Verlag

Hoops, J. (1973-) *Reallexikon der germanischen Altertumskunde*, 2nd. ed. by H. Beck and others, Walter de Gruyter

Hore, H. (1858) 'Irish bardism in 1561', *Ulster Journal of Archaeology* 6, 165-7 and 202-12

Howlett, D. (1974) 'Form and genre in *Widsith', English Studies* 55, 505-11

Hubert, H. (1932) *Les Celtes*, Trubner Verlag

Hughes, K. (1972) *Early Christian Ireland. Introduction to the sources*, Methuen

Hull, V. (1931-4) 'The conception of Conchobor', in *Irish texts*, ed. J. Fraser et al., Sheed and Ward

Jackson, K. (1938) *Cathe Maighe Lena*, Medieval and Modern Irish Series IX, Stationery Office

-- (1964) *The oldest Irish tradition. A window on the Iron Age*, Carnbridge University Press

James, E. (1988) *The Franks*, Basil Blackwell

James, M.R. (1917) 'Two Lives of St. Ethelbert, king and martyr', *English Historical Review* 32, 214-44

Jarnut, J. (1982) *Geschichte der Langobarden*, Urban Taschenbucher

Jones, H. (1917-32) *The geography of Strabo*, Loeb Classical Library, Heinemann

Jones, W. R. (1971) 'The image of the barbarian in medieval Europe', *Comparative Studies in History and Society* 13, 376-404

Kelleher, J. (1963) 'Early Irish history and pseudo-history', *Studia Hibernica* 3, 113-27

-- (1968-9) 'The pre-Norrnan Irish genealogies', *Irish Historical Studies* 16, 138-53

Kelly, F. (1988) *A guide to early Irish law*, Dublin Institute for Advanced Studies

Kenney, J. *The sources for the early history of Ireland: ecclesiastical*, Columbia University Press

Keynes, S. & Lapidge, M. (1983) *Alfred the Great*, Penguin Books.

Kiernan, K. (1996) *Beowulf and the Beowulf Manuscript*, Revised edition, University of Michigan Press

Klaeber, f. (1950) *Beowulf and the Fight at Finnsburg*, Third ed, D.C. Heath & Company

Knott. E. (1916) 'Why Mongan was deprived of noble issue', *Eriu* 8, 155-60

--(1922-6) *The bardic poems of Tadhg Dall O hUiginn*, Irish Text Society 22, 23

Koestermann, E. (1965) *Cornelius Tacitus. Annales*, Teubner

Krapp, G. and Dobbie, E. (1936) *The Exeter Book*, Anglo-Saxon Poetic Records 3, Columbia University Press

Kruger, B. (1983) *Die Germanen. Geschichte und Kultur der germanischen Stamme in Mitteleuropa*, Akademie-Verlag Berlin

Krusch, B. (1888) *Fredegarii et aliorum chronica*, Monumenta Germaniae Historica. Scriptores rerum merovingicarum 2

Krusch, B. & Levison, W. (1951) *Gregorii episcopi Turonensis libri historiarum X*, Monumenta Germaniae Historica. Scriptores rerum merovingicarum 1

Kuhn, F. (1973) *Asen*, In *Reallexikon der germanischen Altertumskunde*, 2nd ed., ed. H. Beck, Walter de Gruyter

Leo, F. (1881) *Venanti Honori Clementiani Fortunati Opera Poetica*, Monumenta Germaniae Historica. Auctores antiquissimi 4

Le Roux, F. (1959) 'A propos du *vergobretus* gaulois. La *regia potestas* en Irlande et en Gaule', *Ogam* 11, 66-80

-- (1986) *Les druides*, 4th ed., Ouest-France

Mac Airt, S. (1958) 'Filidecht and *coimgne*', *Eriu* 18, 139-52

Mac Airt, S. & Mac Niocaill, G. (1983) *The Annals of Ulster (to AD 1131)*, Dublin Institute for Advanced Studies

Macalister, R. (1938-56) *Lebor Gabala Erenn*, Irish Text Society

Mac Cana, P. (1955-56) 'Aspects of the theme of king and goddess in Irish literature', *Etudes Celtiques* 7, 76-144, 356-413 and 8, 59-65

-- (1966) 'On the use of the term *retoiric*', *Celtica* 7, 65-90

-- (1970) 'The three languages and the three laws', *Studia Celtica* 5, 62-78

-- (1972a) 'Conservation and innovation in early Celtic literature', *Etudes Celtiques* 13, 61 - 119

-- (1972b) 'Mongan mac Fiachnai and *Immram Brain*', *Eriu* 23, 102-42

-- (1974) 'The rise of the later schools of *filidheacht*', *Eriu* 25, 126-46

McCone, K. (1986) 'Dubthach maccu Lugair and a matter of life and death in the pseudo-historical prologue to the *Senchas Mar*', *Peritia* 5, 1-35

-- (1989) 'Zur Frage der Register im frühen irischen', *in Early Irish Literature. Media and Communication*, ed. S. Tranter & H. Tristram, Gunter Narr Verlag

-- (1990) *Pagan past and Christian present in early Irish literature*, An Sagart

Mac Eoin, G. (1989) 'Orality and literacy in some Middle Irish King-tales', *in Early Irish Literature. Media and Communication*, ed. S. Trauter and H. Tristram, Gunter Narr Verlag

Mac Niocaill, G. (1972) *Ireland before the Vikings*, Gill and Macmillan

-- (1975) *The medieval Irish annals*, Dublin

MacSweeney, P. (1904) *Caithreim Congail Clairinghnigh*, Irish Text Society

Mallory, J. & Stockman, G. (1994) *Ulidia, Proceedings of the First International Conference on the Ulster Cycle of Tales*

Malone, K. (1962) *Widsith*, Anglistica 13, Rosenkilde and Bagger

-- (1977) *Deor*, Manchester University Press

Manitius, M. (1911) *Geschichte der lateinischen Literatur des Mittelalters*, C.H. Beck Verlag

Martin, R. (1981). *Tactius*, Batsford

Meid, W. (1974) 'Dichtkunst, Rechtspflege, und Medizin im alten Irland', in *Antiquitates Indogermanicae*, ed. M. Mayrhofer, Institut für Sprachwissenschaft der Universität Innsbruck

Meissburger, G. (1963) 'Zum sogenannten Heldenliederbuch Karls des Grossen', *Germanisch-Romanische Mitteilungen* 44, 105-19

Menghin, W. (1985) *Die Langobarden. Archäologie und Geschichte*, Konrad Theiss Verlag

Meroney, H. (1950-58) 'Studies in early Irish satire', *Journal of Celtic Studies* 1, 2

Meyer, K. (1895-7) *The Voyage of Bran*, D. Nutt

-- (1899) 'The song of the sword of Cerball *Revue Celtique* 20, 7-12

-- (1901) 'The expulsion of the Dessi', Y *Cymmrodor* 14, 101 -35

-- (1906) *The death tales of the Ulster heroes*, Todd Lecture Series 14, Max Niemeyer Verlag

-- (1908) 'A poem by Dallan mac More', *Revue Celtique* 29, 210-14

-- (1910) 'Conall Corc and the Corco Luigde', *in Anecdota from Irish Manuscripts*, ed. O. Berin, et al. Dublin

-- (1913) 'Über die älteste irische Dichtung I', *Abhandlungen der königlich preussischen Akademie der Wissenschaften* 6

-- (1914) 'Über die älteste irische Dichtung II', *Abhandlungen der königlich preussischen Akademie der Wissenschaften* 10.

-- (1917) 'Miscellanea Hibernica', *University of Illinois Studies in Language and Literature* 2

-- (1918) 'Mitteilungen aus irischen Handschriften: allerlei Rechtssprüche', *Zeitschrift für celtische Phililogie* 12, 361-6

-- (1919) 'Bruchstücke der älteren Lyrik Irlands', *Abhandlungen der preussischen Akademie der Wissenschaften* 7

Moisl, H. (1979) 'Anglo-Saxon royal genealogies and Germanic oral tradition', *Journal of Medieval History* 7, 215-48.

-- (1981) 'A sixth-century reference to the British *bardd*', *Bulletin of the Board of Celtic Studies* 29, 269-73

-- (1987) 'The Church and the native tradition of learning in early medieval Ireland', in *Irland und die Christenheit*, ed. M. Richter & P. Ni Chathain, Klett-Cotta

184

Mommsen, T. (1882) *Iordanis Romana et Getica,* Monumenta Germaniae Historica. Auctores antiquissimi 5

-- (1894) *Cassiodori Senatoris Variae,* Monumenta Germaniae Historica. Auctores antiquissimi 12

Much, R. (1967) *Die Germania des Tacitus,* Third ed. by W. Lange, Carl Winter Verlag

Mulchrone, K. (1939) *Bethu Phatraic,* Dublin

Murphy, G. (1952) 'On the dates of two sources used in Thurneysen's *Heldensage',* Eriu 16, 145-56

Musset, L. (1975) *The Germanic Invasions,* trans. E. & C. James, Paul Elek

Mytum, H. (1992) *The origins of early Christian Ireland,* Routledge

Nash, D. (1979) 'Reconstructing Poseidonios' Celtic Ethnography: some considerations', *Britannia* 7, 111-26

Newton, S. (1993) *The origins of Beowulf and the pre-Viking kingdom of East Anglia,* D.S. Brewer

Nyberg, T. (1985) *History and heroic tale,* Odense University Press

O'Brien, M. (1939) 'The oldest account of the raid of the Collas', *Ulster Journal of Archaeology* 2

-- (1962) *Corpus genealogiarum Hiberniae,* Dublin Institute for Advanced Studies

O Coileain, S. (1981) 'Some problems of story and history', *Eriu* 32, 115-136

O Corrain, D. (1972) *Ireland before the Vikings,* Gill and Macmillan

-- (1973) 'Dal Cais --church and dynasty', *Eriu* 24, 52-63

-- (1981) 'The early Irish Churches: some aspects of organisation', in *Irish Antiquity,* ed. D. O Corrain, Four Courts Press

-- (1984a) 'Irish law and canon law', in *Irland und Europa,* ed. P. Ni Chathain & M. Richter, Klett-Cotta

185

-- (1985) 'Irish origin legends and genealogy', in Nyberg 1985

-- (1986) 'Historical need and literary narrative', *Proceedings of the Seventh International Congress of Celtic Studies, Oxford 1983*, ed. D. Ellis Evans, J. Griffith, E. Jope

-- (1987) 'Irish vernacular law and the Old Testament', in *Irland und die Christenheit*, ed. M. Richter & P. Ni Chatchain, Klett-Cotta

O Corrain, D., Breatnach, L., Breen, A. (1984b) 'The laws of the Irish', *Peritia* 3, 382-438

O Croinin, D. (1995) *Early medieval Ireland*, Longman

O Cuiv, B. (1963) 'Literary creation and Irish historical tradition', *Proceedings of the British Academy* 49, 233-62

O'Daly, M. (1975) *Cath Maige Mucrama*, Irish Text Society

O'Donnell, J. (1979) *Cassiodorus*, University of California Press

Ogilvie, J. (1963) 'Mimi, scurrae, histriones: entertainers ofthe early middle ages', *Speculum* 38, 603-19

Ogilivie, R. (1967) *De vita Agricolae*, Clarendon Press

Oldfather, C. (1933-67) *Diodorus Siculus*, Loeb Classical Library, Heinemann

Opland, J. (1976) '*Beowulf* on the poet', *Medieval Studies* 38, 442-67

-- 'From horseback to monastic cell: the impact on English literature of the introduction of writing', in *Old English literature in context*, ed. J.D. Niles, Cambridge University Press

-- (1980b) *Anglo-Saxon oral poetry*, Yale University Press.

O'Rahilly, C. (1961) *The Stowe version of Tain Bo Cuailnge*, Dublin Institute for Advanced Studies

-- (1976) *Tain Bo Cuailnge. Recension 1*, Dublin Institute for Advanced Studies

-- (1946) *Early Irish history and mythology*, Dublin Institute for Advanced Studies

Parkes, M. (1976) 'The paleography of the Parker Manuscript of the Chronicle, Laws, and Sedulius, and historiography at Winchester in the late ninth and tenth centuries', *Anglo-Saxon England* 5, 149-71

Partee. B., ter Meulen, A., Wall, R. (1990) *Mathematical methods in linguistics*, Kluwer Academic

Peiper, R. (1883) *Alcimi Ecdicii Aviti Viennensis episcopi opera*, Monumenta Germaniae Historica. Auctores antiquissimi 6

Pertz, G. (1829) *Thegani Vita Hludowici imperatoris*, Monumenta Germaniae Historica. Scriptorum 2

-- (1868) *Rothari Edicti prologus*, Monumenta Germaniae Historica. Leges 4

Pitman, J. (1993) *Probability*, Springer Verlag

Plummer, C. (1910) *Vitae sanctorum Hiberniae*, Oxford University Press

Pokorny, J. (1959) *Indogermanisches etymologisches Worterbuch*, Francke Verlag

Popper, K. (1959) *The logic of scientific discovery*, Hutchinson

-- (1963) *Conjectures and refutations*, Routledge & Kegan Paul

-- (1970) *Objective knowledge*, Clarendon Press.

Quiggin, E. (1911-12) 'Prolegomena to the study ofthe later Irish bards, 1200-1500', *Proceedings of the British Academy* 5, 89-142

Raftery, B. (1984) *La Tene in Ireland*, Veröffentlichungen des vorgeschichtlichen Seminars Marburg, Sonderband 2

Rankin, D. (1995) 'The Celts through Classical eyes', in Green 1995

Richter, M. (1988) *Medieval Ireland. The enduring tradition*, Macmillan

-- (1994) *The formation of the medieval West*, Four Courts Press

Robinson, F. (1912) 'Satirists and enchanters in early Irish literature', in *Studies...presented to C. Toy*, New York

Rolfe, J. (1935) *Ammianus Marcellinus*, Loeb Classical Library, Heinemann

Ross, A. (1995) 'Ritual and the druids', in Green 1995

Rugullis, S. (1982) *Die barbaren in den spätrömischen Gesetzen*, Peter Lang Verlag

Sawyer, P (1978) *From Roman Britain to Norman England*, Methuen

Sawyer, P. & Wood, I. (1977) *Early Medieval Kingship*, University of Leeds Press

Schneider, H. (1962) *Germanische Heldensage*, 2nd ed, Walter de Gruyter

von See, K. (1964) 'Skop und Skald. Zur Auffassung des Dichters bei den Germanen', *Germanisch-romanische Monatsschrift* 14, 1-14

-- (1971) *Germanische Heldensage*, Athenäum Verlag

Seel, O. (1961) *Commentarii rerum gestarum, C. Iulii Caesaris*, Teubner

Shafer, A.J. (1974) *A guide to historical method*, 2nd ed. Dorsey Press

Shippey, T. (1976) *Poems of widsom and learning*, Cambridge University Press

Simpson, J. & Weiner, E. (1989) *The Oxford English Dictionary*, 2nd ed., Clarendon Press

Sisam, K. (1953) 'Anglo-Saxon royal genealogies', *Proceedings of the British Academy* 39, 287-348

Sjoestedt, M. (1926-7) 'Le siege de Druim Damhghaire', *Revue Celtique* 43, 1-123 and *Revue Celtique* 44, 157-86

Smith, R. (1931-4) 'Urchuillti Bretheman', in *Irish Texts*, ed. J. Fraser, vol. 4, Sheed and Ward

Smyth, A. (1972) 'The earliest Irish annals', *Proceedings of the Royal Irish Academy* 72, 1-48

von den Steinen (1932-3) 'Chlodwigs Ubergang zum Christentum', *Mitteilungen des osterreichischen Instituts fur Geschichtsforschung*, Erganzungsband 12, 417-501

Stenton, F. (1971) *Anglo-Saxon England*, 3rd ed., Oxford University Press

Stevenson, W. (1904) *Asser's Life of King Alfred*, Clarendon Press.

Stokes, W. (1862) *Three Irish Glossaries*, Williams and Norgate

-- (1892) 'Echtra Cormaic i Tir Tairngiri', in *Irische Texts*, ed. W. Stokes & E. Windisch. 3rd ser. l, S. Hirzel Verlag

-- (1894) 'The prose tales ofthe Rennes dindsenchas', *Revue Celtique* 15, 272-336, 418-84, and *Revue Celtique* 16, 31-83, 135-67, 269-312

-- (1897) 'Coir Anmann', in *Irische Texts*, ed. W. Stokes & E. Windisch. 3rd ser. 2, S. Hirzel Verlag

-- (1898-1900) 'The Bodleian Amra Choluim Chille', *Revue Celtique* 20, 30-55, 132-83, 248-89, 400-437 and *Revue Celtique* 21, 133-36

-- (1900) 'Da Choca's hostel', *Revue Celtique* 21, 149-65, 312-27, 388-402

-- (1902) 'The death of Muirchertach mac Erca', *Revue Celtique* 23, 395-437

-- (1903) 'The death of Crimthann son of Fidach and the adventures of the sons of Eochu Mugmedon', *Revue Celtique* 24, 172-207

-- (1905) 'The Colloquy of the Two Sages', *Revue Celtique* 26, 4-64

Stokes, W. & Strachan, J. (1901-3) *Thesaurus Paleohibernicus*, Cambridge University Press

Stubbs, W. (1887-9) *Gesta Regum Anglorum*, Rolls Series. 2 vols

Swanton, M. (1970) *The Dream of the Rood*, Manchester University Press

Tangl, M. (1916) *S. Bonifatii et Lulli Epistolae*, Monumenta Germaniae Historica. Epistolae selectae 1

Thomson, R. (1987) *William of Malmesbury*, Boydell Press.

Thurneysen, R. (1891) 'Mittelirische Verslehren', in *Irishe Texte*, ed. W. Stokes and E. Windisch, 3rd ser. 1, S. Hirzel Verlag

-- (1912) 'Zu irischen handschriften und Literarturdenkmälern', *Abhandlungen der königlichen Gesellschaft der Wissenschaften zu Göttingen* 14

189

-- (1921) *Die irische Helden- und Königsage bis zum siebzehnten Jahrhundert,* Max Niemeyer Verlag

-- (1924-5) 'Aus dem irischen Recht III', *Zeitschrift für celtische Philologie* 15, 302-70

-- (1926-7) 'Aus dem irischen Recht IV', *Zeitschrift für celtische Philologie* 16, 167-230

-- (1927) 'Zu Verslehre II' , *Zeitschrift für celtische Philologie* 17, 263-76

-- (1931-3) 'Colman mac Leneni und Senchan Torpeist', *Zeitschrift für celtische Philologie* 19, 193-209

-- (1932) Imbas-for-osndai. Zeitschrift für celtische Philologie 19, 163-4

Tierney, J. (1960) 'The Celtic Ethnography of Posidonius', *Proceedings of the Royal Irish Academy* 60, 189-275

Todd, M. (1987) *The Northern Barbarians 100 BC - AD 300,* revised ed., Basil Blackwell

Tully, J. (ed.) (1988) *Meaning and Context,* Polity Press

Uecker, H. (1972) *Germanische Heldensage,* J.B. Metzler Verlag

Ullmann, W. (1966) *Principles of government and politics in the Middle Ages,* 2nd ed., Methuen

Vansina, J. (1985), *Oral tradition as history,* University of Wisconsin Press

Voretsch, C. (1896) 'Das Merowingerepos und die fränkische Heldensage', *Philologische Studien. Festgabe für Eduard Sievers,* Max Niemeyer Verlag

de Vries, J. (1961) *Keltische Religion,* W. Kohlhammer Verlag

Wagner, H. (1975) 'Studies in the origins of early Celtic traditions', *Eriu* 26, 1-26

-- (1977) 'The archaic Dind Rig poem and related problems', *Eriu* 28, 1-16

Waitz, G. (1878) *Scriptores rerum Langobardicarum et Italicarum, saec. VI-IX,* Monumenta Germaniae Historica

-- (1911) *Einhardi Vita Karoli Magni*, Monumenta Germaniae Historica. Scriptores rerum germanicarum 25

Wallace-Hadrill, J. (1971*)* *Early Germanic kingship in England and on the Continent*, Oxford University Press.

Ward, D. (1973) 'On the poets and poetry of the Indo-Europeans', *Journal of IndoEuropean Studies* 1, 127-44

Wareman, P. (1951) *Spielmannsdichtung: Versuch einer Begriffsbestimmung*, Amsterdam

Wasserschleben, H. (1885) *Die irische Kanonensammlung*, Leipzig

Watson, J. (1941) *Mesca Ulad*, Stationery Office

Wenskus, R. (1961) *Stammesbildung und Verfassung*, Böhlau Verlag

-- (1976) 'Zum Problem der Ansippung', in *Festgabe für Otto Höfler*, ed. H. Birkhan, W. Braumüller Verlag

Werlich, E. (1967) 'Der westgermanische Skop', *Zeitschrift für deutsche Philologie* 86, 352-75

Whickham, C. (1981) *History of the Lombards*, Longman

White, H. (1912) *Appian's Roman History*, Loeb Classical Library, Heinemann

Whitelock, D. (1957) *The Audience of Beowulf*, Oxford University Press

-- (1967) *Sweet's Anglo-Saxon Reader*, Oxford University Press

Wilson, R.M. (1971) *The lost literature of medieval England*, Methuen.

Windisch, E. (1897) 'Tochmarc Ferbe', in *Irische Texte*, ed. W. Stokes & E. Windisch. 3rd ser 2, S. Hirzel Verlag

Windsor, P. (1990) *Reason and History*, Leicester University Press

de Winterfeld, P. (1899) *Poaetae Latini aevi Carolini*, Monumenta Germaniae Historica. Poetae latinae medii aevi 4

Wissmann, W. (1954) 'Skop', *Sitzungsberichte der deutschen Akademie der Wissenschaften zu Berlin* 2, 1-30

Wolfram, H. (1967) 'Intitulatio I. Lateinische Königs- und Fürstentitel bis zum Ende des 8. Jahrhunderts', Mitteilungen der österreichischen Gesellschaft für Geschichtsforschung, Ergänzungsband 21, 99- 103

-- (1968) 'Methodische Fragen zur Kritik am "sakralen" Königtum germanischer Stämme', in *Festschrift für Otto Höfler*, ed. H. Birkhan and O. Gschwantler, Verlag Notring

-- (1970) 'The shaping of the early medieval kingdom', *Viator* 1, 1-20

-- (1971) 'The shaping of the early medeival principality as a type of nonroyal rulership', *Viator* 2, 33-51

-- (1975a) 'Athanaric the Visigoth: monarchy or judgeship. A study in comparative history', *Journal of Medieval History* 1, 259-278

-- (1975b) 'Gotische Studien I. Das Richtertum Athanarichs', *Mitteilungen der österreichischen Gesellschaft für Geschichtsforschung* 83, 1-32

-- (1975c) 'Gotische Studien II. Die terwingische Stammesverfassung und das Bibelgotische (1)', *Mitteilungen der österreichischen Gesellschaft für Geschichtsforschung* 83, 289-324

-- (1977) 'Theogonie, ethnogenese, und ein kompromittierter Grossvater in Stammbaum Theodorichs des Grossen', *in Festschrift für Helmut Beumann*, ed. K. Jaschke and R. Wenskus, Thorbecke Verlag

-- (1979) 'Gotisches Königtum und römisches Kaisertum von Theodosius dem Grossen bis Justinian I', *Frühmittelalterliche Studien* 13, 1 -28

-- (1980) *Geschichte der Goten*, 2nd ed, C.H. Beck Verlag

-- (1981) 'Gothic history and historical ethnography', *Journal of Medieval History* 7, 309-19

-- (1983a) 'Zur Ansiedlung reichsangehöriger Föderaten', *Mitteilungen der österreichischen Gesellschaft für Geschichtsforschung* 91, 5-35

-- (1983b) 'Die Aufnahme germanischer Völker im Römerreich', *Settimane di Studio* 29, 87-117

-- (1990) *Das Reich und die Germanen. Zwischen Antike und Mittelalter*, Siedler Verlag

192

-- (1995) *Die Germanen*, C.H. Beck

Wormald, P. (1977) '*Lex scripta* and *verbum regis*: legislation and Germanic kingship from Euric to Cnut', in Early *Medieval Kingship*, ed. P. Sawyer & I. Wood, published by the editors

-- (1978) 'Bede, *Beowulf*, and the conversion of the Anglo-Saxon aristocracy', in *Bede and Anglo-Saxon England*, ed. R. Farrell, British Archaeological Reports 46, 32-95

6. INDEX

STUDIES IN CLASSICS

oratively by an international panel of experts on economic
tion. Similar calls have been made by others in this volume (see
on *et al*, Chapter 6).

is chapter, the background of economic evaluations and the need for
atic reviews is described, as well as the importance of guideline
pment, in this area. Criteria lists are then distinguished from
nes, before going on to describe the development of a criteria list.
pment of the list is described in two further sections – one in which
g guidelines are compared and one in which a Delphi survey is used.
, some conclusions are drawn, based on the research so far, and
oints for further research are noted.

ground

omic evaluations are a relatively recent phenomenon. Although
preliminary attempts to assess the benefits of possible health care
ntions in economic terms were made in earlier centuries, economic
ions or medical technology assessments, as they are currently
ned, date only to the early 1970s. Economic evaluation is supposed
duce information that might lead to better economic decisions,
g that scarce resources in health care are allocated in the most
t way. Although economic evaluation is designed to support decision
, the actual influence of economic evaluation in policy decisions
much to be desired. One of the reasons for this suboptimal use of
tion from economic evaluations is the use of a variety of
ologies in different studies, which hampers comparability between
 Therefore, a good deal of effort has been put into the development
ardised methods for economic evaluations. At present, textbooks[1] and
us books[2] exist, and numerous country-specific (pharmacoeconomic)
les provide detailed recommendations on how best to perform an
ic evaluation. Although there is consensus on major issues related
omic evaluations, recent debates in the literature have shown that
ments still persist on many other issues (for example, on the
ment of production loss, the use of utility assessments and/or
ess to pay).

lines can serve many purposes.[3] First, guidelines can be linked to
 requirement to provide economic data before a new technology is
d. The development and application of pharmacoeconomic
es is an important example in this category. Second, guidelines can
hodological standards that researchers should meet in making
ic evaluations. Finally, guidelines could contain ethical standards
ractice of economic evaluation (good economic practice analogous
clinical practice).

her development is the intensified use of systematic reviews and
alyses to summarise knowledge and provide "state-of-the-art"

of one of the basic rules of research: evaluation of an intervention must be
based on its objectives. Even when QoL measures were included, the
variety of ad hoc measures developed or used in the studies made any
direct comparison impossible. Although some studies were carried out
before the development of a complete colorectal cancer-specific measure
(the EORTC QLQ-C30), its present availability makes its use in any future
studies a sensible step. Second, all studies were carried out in, or focused
on, identical settings (oncology units) characterised by high capital and
revenue costs. The studies addressed the minimisation of morbidity and
mortality for what is now a highly prevalent disease in Western society
and the third largest cause of cancer death in the UK and the rest of the
developed world. Given the incomplete nature of the evidence presented it
is debatable whether any more investment in tertiary care infrastructure
should be contemplated until good evidence of effect is available.

Conclusions

The conclusions of this chapter must remain tentative given the relative
lack of coverage of the databases used. However, the belief of the authors is
that the evidence presented points to major gaps in the conduct and
reporting of economic evaluations and among these one of the major areas
for improvement is that of the assessment of effectiveness of the interventions
evaluated. While it is possible that single RCTs or reviews of RCTs may not
have been available at the time of the conduct of the economic evaluation, a
significant proportion of evaluations rely on estimates of effect derived from
single, small, non-randomised studies or, possibly even worse, expert
opinion. This is not an ethically defensible practice if better quality estimates
of effect were available at the time the study was conducted. The research
community should take urgent steps to rectify or ameliorate the problem.

Summary points

- When available, good quality evidence from systematic reviews of
  effectiveness should be used in economic evaluation.
- The quality of primary research combined in systematic review is often
  insufficient to address economic issues.

References

1 Drummond MF, Cooke J, Walley T. Economic evaluation in healthcare decision-making:
  evidence from the UK. Centre for Health Economics Discussion Paper. University of
  York, 1996.
2 Elixhauser A. Health care cost-benefit analysis and cost-effectiveness analysis. From 1979
  to 1990: a bibliography. *Med Care* 1993;**31**:JS1–150.
3 Elixhauser A, Halpern M, Schmier J, Luce BR. Health care CBA and CEA from 1991 to
  1996: an updated bibliography. *Med Care* 1998;**36**:MS1–147.

4 Udvarhelyi IS, Colditz GA, Rai A, Epstein AM. Cost-effectiveness and cost-benefit analyses in the medical literature. Are the methods being used correctly? *Ann Intern Med* 1992;**116**:238–44.

5 Gerard K. Cost-utility in practice: a policy maker's guide to the state of the art. *Health Policy* 1992;**21**:249–79.

6 Adams M, McCall N, Gray D, Orza M, Chalmers TC. Economic analysis in randomised controlled trials. *Med Care* 1992;**30**:231–8.

7 Jefferson T, Demicheli V. Is vaccination against hepatitis B efficient? A review of world literature. *Health Econ* 1994;**3**:25–37.

8 Hill SR, Mitchell AS, Henry DA. Problems with the interpretation of pharmacoeconomic analyses: a review of submissions to the Australian Pharmaceutical Benefits Scheme. *JAMA* 2000;**283**:2116–21.

9 Jefferson TO, Demicheli V. The quality of systematic reviews of economic evaluations in healthcare and what they are telling us: it is time for action. Presented at Fourth International Congress on Peer Review and Global Communication, Barcelona, 2001.

10 Drummond MF, Jefferson TO and the BMJ Economic Evaluation Working Party. Guidelines for authors and peer reviewers of economic submissions to the *BMJ*. *BMJ* 1996;**313**:275–83.

11 Drummond M, Brandt A, Luce B, Rovira J. Standardizing methodologies for economic evaluation in health care. Practice, problems, and potential. *Int J Technol Assess Health Care* 1993;**9**:26–36.

12 Drummond MF. *Economic analysis alongside controlled trials: an introduction for clinical researchers*. London: Department of Health, 1994.

13 Kunz R, Oxman AD. The unpredictability paradox: review of empirical comparisons of randomised and non-randomised clinical trials. *BMJ* 1998;**317**:1185–90.

8: Criteria list for conducting system. reviews based on e evaluation studies CHEC project

ANDRE AMENT, SILVIA EVER
GOOSSENS, HENRICA DE VE
VAN TULDER

Introduction

Health care professionals, consumers, research be overwhelmed by the sometimes unmanageal on the effectiveness and efficiency of health car reviews of these studies can help in making which intervention to adopt. For maximum use of economic evaluations should be consisten quality and informative. In this chapter, the ☑ C this project aims to develop a criteria list for syst evaluations. The criteria list contains a minimu be mentioned in every systematic review rega those individual economic evaluations being widely accepted by the scientific community, t

---

* The ☑ CHEC project is a cooperative effort of the De Policy and Economics of Maastricht University, the Inst Hoensbroek, and the Institute for Research in Extramural Medical Centre, Amsterdam.

evidence in a certain area.[4] A systematic review produces an overview of studies (usually selected from the published literature) on a specific topic and synthesising summaries and conclusions on therapeutic effectiveness, diagnostic information, or aetiological and prognostic factors. Systematic reviews usually contain qualitative information, accounting for the methodological quality of the included studies. Meta-analysis is the quantitative method of combining the results of studies on a specific topic (also called statistical pooling). The results of the individual studies are statistically combined to provide an overall measure or pooled estimate of the (cost-)effectiveness of a health care intervention.

Originally, the methodology of performing systematic reviews comes from the field of psychology. Health care methodologists, like biostatisticians and epidemiologists, took the initiative in developing and adapting the methods of systematic reviews in the field of health care. They developed statistical methods for pooling data from different research settings. They also developed a methodology to assess the quality of the studies performed, using criteria for quality.[5,6] In reviewing the existing literature, one finds in many cases studies that show more or less conflicting results. The consequent challenge is to consider and take into account the validity of the individual studies, and come to a final conclusion on the overall outcome.

This process of meta-analysis and systematic review of RCTs on effectiveness, including assessment of the quality of the individual studies, has become a well-developed area in the field of clinical studies over the past ten years. Criteria for quality encompass both internal validity (design, conduct and analysis) and external validity (generalisability). Furthermore, the quality of reporting is important as the reviews are usually based on published studies. Moher and colleagues showed that poor reporting is associated with overestimation of treatment effects.[5,6]

A large number of instruments exist to assess the methodological quality of effect studies.[5,6] Best known are the criteria list developed by Thomas Chalmers[7], the Jadad list[8] and the Delphi list by Verhagen.[9] One study compared 25 different instruments for assessing the quality of RCTs by applying them to one review.[10] The results differed substantially, indicating that the content of the criteria list influences the outcome and is therefore of utmost importance.

Although a large number of systematic reviews of economic evaluations have been performed to date, the methodology in this field is less well developed. One of the reasons is that economic evaluation studies may be even more diverse than effectiveness studies. A number of guidelines for assessing the quality of economic evaluations in systematic reviews have been developed and published. One of these lists was developed by members of the ☑ CHEC project and was used in several systematic reviews of economic evaluations.[11-14] Common problems encountered in these systematic reviews arose from the low number of available studies, the low quality of the data and the poor methodology used within these studies. Regarding the quantity, it was striking that, in general, despite the increased interest in economic evaluation, rather few full economic evaluation studies have been undertaken. In addition, only a limited number of these studies could be classified as cost-utility studies, using quality-adjusted life years (QALYs) as the outcome measure. As to cost calculations, although it is widely recommended, especially from a societal perspective, to include a wide range of costs, only a few studies included all relevant costs. Furthermore, the methods used for cost measurement and cost valuation were often unclear. Almost all studies were "piggybacked", as appendices to the medical outcome study, with the consequence that a separate power analysis regarding economic outcome parameters was not performed in any of the studies. Based on these observations, the reviews concluded that the quality of the studies included was very low.

The lack of a generally accepted methodology for reviewing the economic literature can be considered one of the primary reasons why economic evaluations do not have much influence on policy making. Consequently the ☑ CHEC project aims to enhance the informativeness of reviews of economic evaluations by developing a criteria list which can be used for a solid systematic review regarding such studies. Such a list could be combined with one of the existing criteria lists for assessing the quality of the clinical part of the studies (usually and preferably the randomised controlled trial), in order to assess the overall methodological quality of the clinical study.

Guidelines, checklists and criteria lists

Guidelines give instructions on how to adequately perform or report a study. A researcher performing a cost-effectiveness analysis (CEA) may use guidelines in designing and conducting a study. A checklist is used after the study has been performed and after the results have been published to see if the study met specific guidelines. Of course, there will be a large overlap between guidelines and checklists for the same type of studies.

Criteria lists are used in systematic reviews to consider the methodological quality of the studies included. The criteria usually relate to the internal validity of the studies, but in some criteria lists external validity items are also included. Obviously, different criteria are relevant to different types of studies and different criteria lists should be used for the methodological quality assessment of, for example, randomised trials, or of economic or observational studies. Again, there may be some overlap between criteria lists and guidelines or checklists in a specific research field, but criteria lists are usually more compact and serve a different purpose. That is, the methodological quality assessed by a criteria list should indicate how high or low the chance is that the results of the study are inaccurate or misleading.

Development of a criteria list for the assessment of the methodological quality of economic evaluations in systematic reviews

General design

The aim of the ☑ CHEC project is to develop a criteria list to be used in systematic reviews of economic evaluation studies, by identifying a minimum set of methodological items that reflect the methodological quality of individual economic evaluation studies. The ultimate goal is to produce a systematic, uniform and sound approach to systematic reviews of economic evaluations, so that readers of systematic reviews have the opportunity to judge the quality of the economic evaluation studies included, and have some insight into the validity and reliability of the outcomes. The ☑ CHEC project will focus on the methodological quality of economic evaluations (for example, costs and effects), because other checklists already focus on the methodological quality of more general aspects of clinical effectiveness studies (see Appendix 8.1).

The criteria list has been developed using the Delphi method. This is a consensus method, making use of experts who give written opinions and arguments on a specific problem. These arguments are exchanged among the members of the Delphi panel and this process is repeated until consensus is reached or no new information comes up.[15,16]

Choice of experts

A large number of international experts participated in the Delphi panel. First a Task Force Group was formed consisting of seven internationally acknowledged and prominent experts in the field of economic evaluation. This Task Force Group assisted the project team (authors of this chapter) with the composition of the final Delphi panel. Participants for the Delphi panel were selected if they were authors of guidelines or checklists or if they had special expertise in economic evaluation studies. The project team made a first selection, keeping a balance between various countries and research groups. The inclusion of experts from different research settings all over the world was an explicit goal. This was considered essential for reaching broad acceptance and support for the final criteria list. This preliminary list of experts was evaluated by the Task Force Group, which could suggest eliminating or accepting proposed experts or suggest new candidates for the Delphi panel. This procedure resulted in a final list of 17 persons who were invited to the Delphi panel (See Appendix 8.2). The members of the Task Force Group also participated in the Delphi panel, leading to a final complete panel of 24 members.

Selection of items

Items were selected from existing guidelines, checklists and criteria lists regarding cost-effectiveness analysis. Several strategies were combined to identify the relevant literature in the field of economic evaluation. First, a MEDLINE search was performed for the period 1990 to 2000 using MeSH headings "cost and cost analysis", "meta-analysis" or "review literature". Additionally, Psychlit and Econlit were screened for the same period using keywords "review" or "meta-analysis" and "economic" or "cost*" in titles. Additional articles were identified by searching the Cochrane Library (2000, Issue 3) and the NHS EED database using the terms "cost*" or "economic*". Finally, handbooks on economic evaluation studies were monitored and a request to submit additional guidelines was presented to the Healthecon Discussion List.

Analysis of existing guidelines

A total of 25 guidelines were initially identified through the procedure described above (see Appendix 8.3). A closer look revealed that several guidelines were the same and others were inadequate for our goal. Thus, 15 different guidelines (see Table 8.1) were finally included, which were used for the first item selection.

There was still a wide variety among these 15 guidelines. Some of the guidelines aimed at providing information to researchers, others at providing information to journal referees or to authors who intend to submit their study for publication in journals. Some guidelines restricted themselves to about 10 items, using very broadly defined items, whereas other guidelines produced lists of up to 50 detailed items. In Table 8.1 these guidelines are described in more detail. A distinction was made between: (1) guidelines for economic evaluations and (2) guidelines for performing systematic reviews or assessment of published studies.

Six guidelines were developed for economic evaluations and nine for systematic reviews. In general, little attention has been paid to the following aspects: description of target population, follow up period and the independent position of investigators. The first two aspects could be considered methodological aspects. The independence of the investigator seems to be recognised as a relevant factor in some of the more recent guidelines. Aspects covered by many guidelines are standard economic evaluation core issues like: choice of alternatives, perspective, identification measurement and valuation of costs and benefits, discounting, handling of uncertainties and application of incremental analysis.

Designing the Delphi survey

Preparing the questionnaire for the first Delphi round

The initial item pool was constructed using the items of the 15 guidelines (see Table 8.1), so that there was a total of 218 items. Unavoidably, there were many duplicate items and this first item pool was somewhat redundant. The item pool was restructured by: (1) development of a classification scheme and (2) reduction of the item pool.

Table 8.1 Analysis of 15 existing guidelines.

Category	Guidelines for economic evaluation						Guidelines for systematic reviews								
	Adams	Clemens	Detsky	Eisenberg	Gerard	Gold	Bradley Gibson Sacristán	MUHSC Drummond 1996 Drummond 1997	Drummond 1997	Drummond 1993	Evers	Haycox	Lee	Sanchez 1995 Sanchez 1999	Udvarhelyi
1 Description of the target population	×	×		×		×	×	×		×				×	
2 Choice of alternatives	×	×	×	×		×	×	×		×				×	
3 Economic study question		×	×		×		×	×	×	×	×	×	×	×	
4 Economic study design	×		×	×		×	×	×		×	×		×		
5 Follow up period	×	×	×	×	×	×	×			×					
6 Perspective	×	×	×	×	×	×	×	×		×	×			×	×
7 Economic identification	×		×	×				×		×	×		×	×	×
8 Economic measurement	×		×	×				×	×	×	×		×	×	
9 Economic valuation	×		×	×				×	×	×	×		×	×	
10 Outcome identification		×	×		×	×	×	×		×	×		×	×	×
11 Outcome measurement					×	×		×	×	×	×		×		
12 Outcome valuation			×	×	×			×	×	×	×		×	×	
13 Adjustment for time variation	×	×	×	×	×	×	×	×		×	×		×	×	×
14 Sensitivity and uncertainties	×	×	×	×	×	×	×	×	×	×	×		×	×	×
15 Presentation of results		×			×	×	×	×		×	×		×	×	×
16 Generalisability of results					×	×		×		×		×		×	
17 Incremental analysis	×	×	×	×		×	×	×	×	×	×		×	×	×
18 Independence of investigators		×	×						×	×				×	
19 Ethics and distribution of effects	×		×	×		×	×	×		×				×	

For references see Appendix 8.3

Development of a classification scheme

To facilitate analysis of the item pool, a classification scheme was developed for the individual items. This classification was a necessary step in order to reduce the number of items in a scientifically justified way, without any loss of information. Three members of the team (SE, MG and AA) developed a classification scheme in a rather open consensus procedure. Starting with broad categories (for example, "costs" and "benefits"), categories were added if new items could not be classified into one of the categories that were used at that moment. If there were many items in one category and subdivision was considered necessary, subcategories were created. For example, the category "costs" was subdivided into the classes "identification of costs", "measurement of costs" and "valuation of costs". Finally, a classification scheme with 19 categories was developed, in which almost all items of the original pool could be classified (see Table 8.1).

However, some items were difficult to classify. When there was no consensus among the three investigators about classification, these items were provisionally put into a separate category labelled "unclear".

Reduction of the item pool

Reduction of items should be performed in a transparent and reproducible way. A two-step method was applied to complete this reduction:

1 Items were first classified into several subcategories. For example, for the subcategory "measuring costs": in some guidelines the item was phrased "How are costs measured?", whereas in other guidelines the question was slightly differently phrased as "Are costs measured appropriately?", and in other guidelines even more specifically "Are costs measured suitably for the perspective?". Careful analysis of the items in the subcategories led to further subdivision. The final items for the first Delphi round were presented using this more refined classification.
2 After classifying the items according to this more detailed system, it became possible to compare more or less similar items directly with each other, which facilitated further reduction of the item pool without any loss of information.

The following strategy was used for item reduction:

1 No items on general methodology (covered by criteria lists of clinical trials).
2 (Almost) identical formulations skipped.
3 More general wording preferred above specific wording.
4 No double questions are allowed.

5 No use of the word "should".

6 "Closed" items are better than "open" items.

7 No unclear, imprecise items.

8 Item must be clear and understandable, without original context.

9 Items must be clear, without examples.

10 Short wording is preferred over extensive wording.

11 Objective items are preferred over subjective items.

12 Present time is preferred over past time in wording.

After applying the above rules to the initial item pool, the number of items reduced from 218 to 128. This set of 128 items was used in the first Delphi round.

Phrasing of answering categories

Of course, the phrasing of the answering categories is related to the way the original questions were phrased. In the original guidelines, all kinds of answering categories were found, and these categories sometimes varied even within one guideline. Although the majority of questions were formulated in a more closed or objective way – asking for dichotomous answers (Yes/No), asking for hard evidence or objective information (for example: "Are costs discounted?") – in many other cases the questions were phrased in a more open or subjective way (for example: "Are costs discounted appropriately?"), with questions asking for interpretations from a broader perspective (for example: "Are costs measured appropriately for the research question?"). Sometimes rather limited enumeration of answering categories was provided; for example, in determining the perspective of the analysis (society, the health care sector, insurers, institutions, clients, other). In other cases, categorical answering categories were used; for example, the item concerning whether costs were measured appropriately could consist of four answering categories: all (all costs are measured appropriately), most, some and none.

In the first Delphi round, we asked the panel only if they considered the items to be relevant as appropriate elements of the criteria list, but did not ask about the specific answering categories.

Design of the first Delphi round

The questionnaire of the first Delphi round was returned by 23 of the 24 experts who were selected for the Delphi panel. The questionnaire consisted of 128 items spread over 19 categories. First, the expert was asked to state for each category whether it should be included in a criteria list of a minimum set of items. Then, the expert was asked to give his or her opinion about the items in each of the categories that they wanted on the list, regarding whether these items should be on the list. Furthermore, it was possible for the expert to give an alternative formulation for an item.

Table 8.2 Responses of the first Delphi round.

Categories	Agreement on inclusion of category (%)	Number of items within each category	Agreement on inclusion of individual items (%)
1 Description of the target population	100	2	55–77
2 Choice of alternatives	100	7	17–91
3 Economic study question	91	2	39–87
4 Economic study design	91	3	26–70
5 Follow up period	100	2	61–83
6 Perspective	100	3	43–78
7 Resource use/input identification	100	11	22–78
8 Resource use/input measurement	96	19	9–57
9 Resource use/input valuation	96	10	9–57
10 Outcome identification	100	10	30–78
11 Outcome measurement	96	8	26–65
12 Outcome valuation	96	4	35–65
13 Discounting/adjustment for time differences	100	7	43–70
14 Sensitivity and uncertainties	100	8	22–78
15 Presentation of results	100	10	30–96
16 Generalisability of results	91	5	17–87
17 Incremental analysis	87	8	13–70
18 Independence of investigators	91	1	83
19 Ethics and distributional effects	83	3	26–61

Results of the Delphi round

The results of the first Delphi round showed that the differences for each category were minimal (see Table 8.2). However, the items did show some obvious differences (see Table 8.2). The experts influenced the analysis, since they judged the items not only in a quantitative way, but also in a qualitative way. The alternative formulations for the items that the experts suggested presented some problems, as a simple quantitative analysis (by using a cut-off point of the percentage of responses) was no longer sufficient. Each separate category of the questionnaire was analysed, to evaluate the percentage as well as the alternative formulations that were suggested by the experts.

In general, there is a high agreement on the categories to be included in the final version of the ☑ CHEC list. This can be concluded from the second column of Table 8.2. For example, all of the experts have the opinion that "Description of the target population" (first category) should be represented in the final criteria list. There is less agreement with regard to item 17, "Incremental analysis" (87%) and 19 "Ethics and distributional effects" (83%).

However, if one looks at the range of the responses on the separate items within each category, there is much less consensus among the experts. This can be seen from the third and fourth columns. For example, category 1 contains two items: in the fourth column there is a range from 55 to77%, which means that 55% of the experts agree on the one item and 77% agree on the other item. In the second Delphi round the focus will be on these differences in order to construct the final criteria list. This is even more complicated because there are also additional suggestions given by some experts in the first round which are not reported on here.

Conclusion and discussions

By creating a criteria list consisting of a minimum set of items, the ☑ CHEC project makes it possible for future systematic reviews of economic evaluations to become more transparent, informative and comparable. Consequently, these systematic reviews might be used more easily by researchers and policy makers. However, the project has some limitations, as follows.

The ☑ CHEC criteria list does not include more general design characteristics of clinical studies, because criteria lists for these aspects have already been published in the international literature. In the future, the ☑ CHEC criteria list might be combined with a criteria list concerning effect studies.[5,7,9]

The possible combination of the ☑ CHEC list with another list raises an additional point. The other lists clearly are only applicable in randomised or non-randomised controlled trials (RCTs and CCTs respectively). Economic evaluations very often do make use of other designs. Use of the ☑ CHEC list in combination with another existing list is therefore limited to full economic evaluations alongside RCTs or CCTs. The RCT design is considered to be the gold standard within the field of evidence-based medicine, but it is widely recognised that in many situations this design cannot be used. Economic evaluations are also based on modelling studies, in which a wide variety of data gathering techniques and data processing models are used. There is still a need to develop an additional checklist for assessing the quality of economic evaluations based on modelling studies or other designs.

Guidelines have been criticised because of their potential rigidity, which might prohibit further development of methodology. This criticism is only valid if guidelines are used injudiciously. To prevent the criteria list from being methodologically rigid, it should be emphasised that this list is a minimum set, with the aim of stimulating researchers to add additional items appropriate for the specific subject under study.

Many of the experts that we asked to participate in the Delphi panel gave their consent. One refused because he was concerned that the development of a criteria list would lead to disregard of low quality studies that might nevertheless contain useful information in some sense, and that sometimes it might be better to base decisions on less optimal information than on no information at all. In this context, it is important to emphasise that the aim of our criteria list is to describe the characteristics of all studies retrieved and not to throw studies away or ignore information. Including quality assessment when using this criteria list may help decision makers (and others) to recognise the validity of the studies and the usefulness of the information.

In order eventually to reach broad acceptance among the scientific community a Delphi panel of widely acknowledged persons was composed. In this chapter the first step of the procedure has been reported; the second Delphi round has yet to be undertaken and it is only after the second step that the final list of criteria will be produced. Additionally, in order to stimulate dissemination of the criteria list a validation procedure of the final list will be undertaken.

Finally, there are many examples of poor reporting in economic evaluation studies. It is often difficult to conclude what actually happened in the study and this affects the methodological quality assessment. A solution could be to contact the authors of the original paper, asking them for a more detailed description of the study design. An alternative would be to require the production of a standard technical report for every economic evaluation study. This technical report should be available for everyone, on the Internet if possible. Such a technical report, describing the economic design of the study, could then be used in the systematic review. The criteria list has the potential to influence the quality of both the performance and the reporting of economic evaluation studies.

Hopefully the ☑ CHEC project will lead to a generally acceptable criteria list for the methodological quality assessment of economic evaluations in systematic reviews. The adoption of such a core set of items by researchers could lead to increased comparability of the results of systematic reviews of economic evaluation studies in the near future.

Appendices

Appendix 8.1: Methodological criteria list for systematic reviews[9]

1 Was a method of randomisation performed?
2 Was the treatment allocation concealed?
3 Were the groups similar at baseline regarding most important prognostic factors?
4 Were the eligibility criteria specified?
5 Was the outcome assessor blinded?
6 Was the care provider blinded?
7 Was the patient blinded?
8 Were point estimates and measures of variability presented for the primary outcome measures?
9 Did the analysis include an intention-to-treat analysis?

Answering categories: Yes/No/Don't know